THE
NOW
TESTAMENT

Cycle B

THE
NOW
TESTAMENT

JOSEPH M. WADOWICZ

This volume features the Sunday
Gospels, according to Matthew and
John, of liturgical cycle B.

"Good News" for the Twenty-First Century

Pentland Press, Inc.
www.pentlandpressusa.com

PUBLISHED BY PENTLAND PRESS, INC.
5122 Bur Oak Circle, Raleigh, North Carolina 27612
United States of America
919-782-0281

ISBN 1-57197-317-6
Library of Congress Control Number: 2002101609

Printed in the United States of America

Tout Comprendre
Tout Pardonner

To understand everything
is to forgive everything.

TABLE OF CONTENTS
(CYCLE B)

FOREWORD

When Father Wadowicz asked me to write the foreword to this volume of pithy homilies, he had no idea the daunting task he was asking of me. And yet because of my deep admiration of his priestly dedication and writing skills, I am honored to have this opportunity.

Ordinarily, affinity to a writer friend would fog objectivity. In this case, however, nothing I write can add or take away from the intrinsic beauty of this collection of homilies.

Writers struggle to achieve Father Wadowicz's consummate way with words, conveying ideas at once deep and colorful.

I once watched a crow repeatedly pick up a walnut, still encased in its fleshy green outer coat, soar upward thirty feet or so and then drop it 'til it finally cracked and yielded its inner morsel. I relate to Father Wadowicz's ability to "break open" the Word of God.

Most of us have heard the same scriptures over and over. We think we understand them. Many of us still think of them in the juvenile way we first heard them. But what is astonishing is that, in whatever time or place they are read, they have a relevance and power at once ancient yet ever new. It is a *living* Word.

Father Wadowicz has that ability to open up the familiar scripture to find the pearl of deeper meaning. His style is modern; his words and ideas current. The scripture becomes a living message that fills the listener and reader with the optimism of faith, hope and love. It really is Good News.

Proclaim the Good News to every creature, Jesus urged. Thank you, Father Wadowicz.

– Emery R. Tang, O.F.M.

INTRODUCTION

Testament means "agreement." It could be extended to mean "love letter." The Old Testament is the recorded understanding between Yahweh and the Hebrews after their Egypt exodus.

The New Testament is an updated accord with the Father through His extraordinary representative, Jesus of Nazareth, who emphasized divine love and forgiveness for the entire world—God's love letter.

Now is another word for "eternal." Now is never over. Now is a perpetual present. *The Now Testament* ventures into its second volume of a trilogy of Sunday Gospel readings for liturgical cycle B. Love, old or new, is forever fresh!

HOMECOMING

It is New Year's Day for the Church—the first Sunday of Advent—as the twentieth century slips farther and farther away. For some, the recent approach of Y2K spelled ominous foreboding. Nor does the gospel today mitigate that tension. . . . "Be watchful! Be alert! . . . You do not know when the time will come! . . . You do not know when the Lord of the house is coming."

Why must this *coming* be seen as a menacing ambush—a snare to the nonvigilant? History records its share of religious vigilantes. St. Paul, for a spell, preached the Lord's Second Coming to be in his own lifetime. Centuries later, a Baptist, Benjamin Leach, predicted the year to be 1689. Methodism's founder, Charles Wesley, pronounced the date to be 1794. An American, William Miller, gathered a flock who sold their possessions, moved to upstate New York and awaited the grand finale in 1846. The passing of the second millennium will no doubt breed its own doomsayers.

The traditional notion of Judgment Day has all the spooky appeal of Poe's "Murders in the Rue Morgue." This hardly jibes with the image of the good Shepherd tenderly rescuing the lost sheep. So, what are we to watch for . . . a hanging judge or a deliverer? The scripture features both—take your pick!

The spirit of the season offers ample opportunity in favor of the latter. Like no other month in the year, December brims with brilliance, color and caroling. The malls are jammed, sales soar, shoppers scurry. It's that magic time again when the focus is on others . . . what gift to get for the folks you care about; what Christmas card says the greeting you feel; what surprise will delight your significant other? People seem more willing to be pried loose from their conventional shyness and enjoy being friendly, convivial, jolly. They like being good-natured. It's liberating!

Then there's the other side to the festival. The perennial complaint that the Yule fuels consumerism; that wide-hearted emotions are outrageously exploited in the holiday hype. The Puritans thought the festal merrymaking a bit much and outlawed Christmas.

Perhaps holly time could be made holy time by preparing a gift list for the birthday child. Nothing extravagant—just things one doesn't need, like temper tantrums, or insisting on having one's own way, or snacking when not even hungry, or working off those extra pounds, or walking those five blocks instead of driving. It's a cozy time—the days shorten and darken—good sleeping weather! But the Advent wake-up call sounds! He has come and we are still becoming.

Virtue cannot be imposed either by authority or by threat. According to Thomas Aquinas, virtue is a habit achieved by repetition. So, Advent can be seen rather as a bidding to be our least constricted selves—good-hearted, congenial, easygoing. Jesus must have been comfortable even in a stable with the warmth of his mother. Maybe even our manger hearts can be another homecoming for him.

MARK TIME?

Of the four Gospels, Mark's is regarded as the shortest, the oldest, the most vigorous and picturesque. He was the son of a well-to-do Jerusalem Jewess whose home was a center for the gathering of Jesus believers (Acts 12:12). His cousin was Barnabas and both of them accompanied Paul on his first missionary journey. For some reason, halfway into the tour, Mark returned home. There may have been a falling out over this, since Barnabas also later quit Paul. All were eventually reconciled. Mark's biography of Jesus reflects, therefore, the insights of Paul and the eyewitness highlights of Peter. The essence of his Gospel is condensed in a single sentence . . . the first one.

According to *The Way*, the Tyndale House version of the Bible: "Here begins the wonderful story of Jesus, the Messiah, the Son of God."

Of course Christ was not Jesus' surname. It is a title of Greek origin which meant "anointed." The Hebrew word for anointed is *messiah*. Special people were anointed, who had a special mission, like kings and prophets. Cyrus, the pagan Persian emperor (529 B.C.E.) was given that designation by the grateful Israelites he had liberated. Especially favored intimates of the Almighty were labeled kin to the Almighty. The prophet Hosea referred to his own people as "sons and children of God" (Hos. 1:10).

The Bible thus ascribes "Messiah" and "Son of God" to more than just Jesus. It is the advance man, John, who clearly proclaims the singular transcendence of Jesus, "I

3

have baptized you with water, but he will baptize you with the Holy Spirit."

What can this mean if not that the baptism of Jesus is more than a religious ritual? It has to mean an inner experience, a heightened awareness of the sacredness of reality: a consecration of the common stuff of life, like making a living, raising a family, sensitivity to humanity. Baptism by the Holy Spirit can mean only one thing: the grace to commit to love. What could more infallibly reflect the presence of the Spirit of God than a compassionate human heart?

The Holy Spirit is the *Good News,* and the core of this message is the practice to be kind rather than right. It consistently communicates that connectedness is the essential component of the human condition. Mankind is a network—a complicated original—that does not survive in isolation. Love is a corporate enterprise and needs to be completely inclusive. The baptism of Jesus invites us beyond the desert of separateness into a fresh field of energy—interrelatedness. Why is human connectedness so important? Because humanity is connected to divinity. Human beings all tread the same earth, warm by the same sun, and breathe the same oxygen as Jesus did. To comfort the discomfited is to be his heart and his hands. Liturgically, Mark will march us into the new millennium. Each week in the final year of the twentieth century he will track the steps of that incomparable life that is a blueprint for our own. Time to be on your Mark!

WHAT'S SO FUNNY?

Life is a mixed bag of fortune cookies. Paul recommends that we lighten up about it. At least life turned around for him on that road to Damascus when Jesus happened to him. It must have been a relief for the Apostle mystic to be full of someone besides himself. Gradually it must have dawned on him that religion was not far-right, or uptight, or even being right. It was not the rigid, rigorous, resentful ritual business it had been for him. It most likely was elating to discover that faith was not something, it was Someone. For Saul this new awareness made him Paul, and with this conversion, the personal conviction that "joy is the infallible sign of the presence of God." His enthusiasm eventually spilled out on the Thessalonians: "Brothers and sisters, rejoice always!"

The well-being that flows from a sound spirituality cannot be commanded, or even intended. Like divine grace it happens, unbidden. Saul/Paul had no idea what would befall him on that fated road. He had other things on his mind when the lightning struck. Suddenly it all changed. He began to have new notions of what was important.

No doubt the unfamiliar meanings took time to ripen. Maybe an unexpected tranquility even mingled with his wonderment and an interior harmony was being forged within Paul. It's like when one experiences getting it together. Heightened awareness and the acceptance of life's ups and downs with equal serenity take place after the numbness.

The Now Testament

Kahlil Gibran (1883-1931) in his tour de force *The Prophet*, captures the counterpoint in the nature of genuine joy:

Your joy is your sorrow unmasked. And the self—same well from which your laughter rises was often times filled with your tears . . . The deeper that sorrow carves into your being, the more joy you can contain.

This sense of at-one-ment with the universe and with oneself sets in when one lets go . . . lets go of whatever fences one in: erroneous education, harsh religion, suspicion of the physical, the pretense to be number one, the pressure to fit in, the preoccupation to please . . .

In this enterprise, humor helps. If joy is the intimate relative of divinity, then humor is its kissing cousin. Humor needs 20/20 vision in order to perceive life's paradox, contradictions, and ambiguities that are laughable. Humor is holy when it has the faith to accept the incongruities of God's Creation. Whatever gladdens, saddens, or maddens the human heart rates a genuflection. Humor is the harmony that can celebrate our eccentricities, our inhibitions, our prohibitions, our hopelessly unrealizable ideals and still smile.

Laughter is healthy. It releases to the bloodstream endorphins, the body's natural pain controller. It provides six times more oxygen to tissues than deep breathing. It aids the heart, opens the pores, enhances respiration, digestion and relaxation. One cannot laugh and be angry at the same time. Someone once called laughing "interior jogging." It comes from the same sensitive, susceptible side of us that makes our tears. It affirms that of all the missing persons in our lives, God is the most missed. Benita, age 10, caught this insight when she wrote:

Dear Mr. God,
Love is a two way street. It's your turn, God.

Humor does not deny tragedy, any more than the clown, who is consistently tricked, humiliated, stepped-on, but never defeated. So, what's so funny? Life, you, me, maybe even God! After all, *She* put this show on the road!

CHEERS!

I was waiting for a bus one December day in the mid-'50s. It was a Santa Monica corner where Henshey's department store was located. Two passers-by gazed at the manger scene in the store's display window. I overheard one say to the other petulantly, "They're trying to put religion into everything."

There are those who need no convincing that Christmas is a particularly apt occasion to justify religious expression, and sadly deplore when Christ is left out of it, or when the *mas* (Mass) part gets shortchanged in the celebration. The commercialization of the festival is gravely lamented by the devout. But can commerce really compete with the spiritual magic of the season? The jingle bells of cash registers cannot successfully drown out the bells of St. Mary's. How does mourning the tide of secularism bring the Savior nearer? Can the Creator ever be separated from His Creation? Does the sun need human perception to keep shining, when hidden by clouds?

There is no way to overlook divinity. Even atheists attest to this reality. . . . cigarettes are needed to have anti-cigarette laws! The Divine Presence is everywhere. The English poet Francis Thompson (1859-1902) saw it sublimely in his poem "The Kingdom of God" . . .

O World invisible, we view Thee.
O World intangible, we touch Thee.
O World unknowable, we know Thee.
In apprehensible, we clutch Thee!

Does the fish soar to find the ocean?
The eagle plunge to find the air.
That we ask of the stars in motion
If they have rumor of Thee there?

The angels keep their ancient places:
Turn but a stone, and start a wing!
Tis ye, tis your estranged faces,
That miss the many splendored thing.

Churches have always assumed the charge of serving as God's official bodyguard. Yet if God revealed Himself principally by theology, then only Ph.D.s would be believers. In this day's first reading, King David feels obliged to take care of God. His edifice complex prompts him to build God a temple. Through Nathan, the Prophet, God's response to David's offer is, in effect, "No thanks, you need it more than I do."

So, Christmas cannot be submerged by any economy—bullish or bearish. Its message is too unearthly. "White Christmas" and "Jingle Bells" are not competing with "Adeste Fidelis" and "Silent Night." They separately, lyrically announce the glad tidings of love and peace. "Rudolph" or "Frosty" or "Santa" may supplement, but never supplant, the Bethlehem Baby.

Christmas urges us to say *Mary's yes* to life, which echoed the *yes* of the Creator when He made the universe, and liked what He had made. Christmas says God has not changed His mind about this. In fact He wants to be here—in the center of it. So, give the gifts, relish family, hug the kids. We raise our glasses to God's world!

HUMAN IS HOLY

While the twentieth century and the second millennium stagger to their respective graves, dare we, U.S.A., swagger to our self-elected grade of world power number one? Superiority complexes usually mask inferiority complexes. As an era ends, a national inventory reveals a few things we may justly feel inferior about.

Our economy booms and so do our senseless murders. Unemployment is down and so are the pink-slipped victims of corporate merger downsizing. The homeless increase and so do the soaring salaries of corporate CEOs. In 1980, the ratio between the salary of a top executive and the wage of a factory worker was 42 to one. In 1998, the figure exploded to 419 to one. Still the needy try to survive on food stamps.

The Cold War is over, but the Pentagon budget currently amounts to one half million a minute. That is $9,000.00 per second, which could pay a lot of college tuitions. And that's not to mention the hundreds of millions that will be squandered this year for political campaigns by candidates that don't even get elected. Votes do not put aspirants into office—money does!

After decades of the draining integrity of our national leadership, fate chose a place called Vietnam to call in our debt. This humiliation has taught us something about the ultimate failure of massive power. Yet the U.S.A. is our home, where opportunity abounds like nowhere else in the world. Where the races can connect, and where diversity stands a chance. All human history is a legend of progress and decline, of crises confronted and solutions achieved. It

11

can be no surprise to the Creator that His creatures are imperfect. That is how we were made—unfinished, in process! That is what creatureliness means—limited! We dangle between the infinite and the infinitesimal. And with it all the Divine spark glimmers unextinguished in all mankind.

Each generation hints that humanity is only getting started. The species is only beginning to get the hang of what it means to be a human being! Jesuit paleontologist, Theilhard DeChardin (1881-1955), caught a glimpse of the mystery: "Someday, after mastering the winds, the waves, the tides, and gravity, we shall harness for God the energies of love, and then, for a second time in the history of the world, man will have discovered fire."

More and more scientists are sensing the hunch that benevolence is the mystic secret underlying the basis of the universe. Happiness may only be a sometime thing for harassed mortals, but evil can never be the bottom line. Human is not an excuse, it's a privilege!

The holy family had their dysfunctional moments, but they are more than a footnote to history. We all belong to a holy family—mankind. We were born holy—each one of us—because we came from the Hand of God. Human is holy! Whatever the future holds, we know who holds the future.

Y2~OK

It was a blast watching TV hopscotch the globe on New Year's Eve 2000. It was a kick to be in on a global party— people enjoying themselves in the sight of the glorious Eiffel Tower, the gleaming Thames, and in Calcutta, Johannesburg, Tokyo, Beijing, and Moscow. It was a break to join in the international countdown to the new millennium with happy celebrants around the wide world. In this colorful diversity, I sensed the majesty of its Creator. Mankind, in all its variegated hues, is the perceptible manifestation of divinity—the Epiphany of God.

What will this new century bring? The first woman U.S. president, automobiles fueled by hydrogen and oxygen, clothing made from anti-bacterial fabrics making deodorants a thing of the past? Painless eye surgery is already eliminating eyeglasses. Computers may make books passé. How about a garage sale for worn out replaced body parts? Will miraculous modern medicine discover cures for cancer, AIDS, the common cold? Improved intelligence and technology hold the promise of undreamed advances for the twenty-first century. State of the art items today threaten to be junk tomorrow.

Problems persist, nonetheless. There is global warming, barely confronted. Folks living at the seashore may need to move to the second floor. War continues to be a national policy. The past century, the bloodiest in human history, records one hundred million dead from this insanity. Civilization and education have not yet liberated mankind from the prison of infectious "isms": nationalism, militarism, materialism, fundamentalism. Ideologies are always dangerous when slogans substitute logic and brainwashing is accepted pedagogy.

Among the agreeable "isms" is optimism—a particularly becoming attitude for a freshly minted millennium. There is solid justification for this as I notice the baby boomers' progeny. The young people born between 1977 and 1994 are seventy million strong, and you parents know that they are brighter, more interesting, more confident, and less apologetic than you may remember yourselves having been. You nurtured them sensitively, respecting their individuality and, thus, they seem more concerned for one another. Socially they are more open. One out of seven among their peers are African-American, one out of seven, Hispanic. Scholastically they are obliged to compete with brilliant Asians who garner the academic prizes. They are more colorblind. They have grown up amid a wider diversity and recognize that women are every bit as competent as men. They have matured with an understanding for gays, for the backward, for the underprivileged. They enjoy social service and are quick to volunteer to build or repair or maintain necessities for the have-nots.

There are always exceptions, and there are some things I will never miss if these youths finally outgrow baggy pants, spiked hair, pierced tongues, tattoos and punk rock. But I trust their unbigoted minds, their willing hearts, their no-nonsense spirituality that values each human being with the importance of Jesus himself. I raise a New Year's toast to you. This is your century!

DECISION, DECISIONS!

Considered to be the first of the Gospels, written between 55 and 70 A.D., Mark moves fast. He makes no mention of Jesus' birth or childhood years, he just has him appear suddenly—out of nowhere—fully grown, recognized and baptized by John as someone special. This again was ratified by a numinous celestial confirmation; Jesus was ready for his new vocation. It took him thirty years to decide to go public.

Decision making can be awesome, especially if the only options are risky. There are moments when we know what we have to do, but are terrified to do it. . . . Should I tolerate the travail of chemotherapy, or take my chances? Should I just quit or confront the badgering boss? Decisions, decisions! The temptation is to retreat, and ever rue playing chicken. Shakespeare's familiar lines from *Julius Caesar*, act 4, scene 3, describe the dilemma:

> There is a tide in the affairs of man,
> Which taken at the flood,
> Leads to fortune.
> Omitted, all the voyage of their
> Lives is bound in shallows
> And in miseries.

An undecided life is a wasted life. A state of constant, rootless, restless drifting. In Apostolic days, baptism meant taking a stand about one's life. It was a "decision for Christ"—the commitment to believe what Jesus believed.

15

The rite of baptism has had a checkered career in Church history. Initially it was exclusively intended for adults capable of free choice. In the fourth century, Augustine picked up on the Pauline Theory that mankind was separated from God due to Adam's noncompliance and "original sin" took hold . . . a tenet that is not biblical, but a later theological development. Baptism was seen as a divine presidential pardon. Hence, its focus began to light on infants in order to qualify them for heaven as soon as possible. By the fifth century the mood about baptism shifted from purposeful conversion to passive amnesty.

The ritual of baptism is meant to signify a bonding—a new alliance with God. That is why it is called "Christ-ening," because Christ stands in for the baptizee, giving that person his (Christ's) identity with the Father. It can be likened to the ceremony of naturalization when an alien is made a citizen of the U.S.A. So important is this formality to the Church that it empowers all believers to perform it, not just its currently endangered species, the ordained priesthood.

There are several kinds of baptism. Baptism of water—the conventional version. When this is not available, there is baptism of blood—suffering for the faith, martyrdom. There is baptism of desire—the wish to conform to God's wishes. Let me tell you about still another variety—the baptism of tears.

> The hospital's student chaplain was on call. Late one night he was summoned to the room of a mother whose baby had been stillborn a few hours earlier. "We want our baby baptized," the young couple asked, the mother cradling the lifeless body of their daughter. "Her name's Nicole."
>
> The inexperienced chaplain didn't know what to do. In order to buy some time, he asked the couple to meet him in the chapel a few minutes later. The

overwhelmed chaplain frantically tried to find a more experienced chaplain to take over, but none was available. So, he was on his own. Despite his nervousness over his professional inexperience and theological uncertainties about what to do, he tried to think of what to say to the grieving parents.

When the couple arrived, the chaplain realized his words would be inadequate. Instead, and almost without realizing it, he took a tissue, wiped at the tears in the eyes of the parents, then wiped his own tears, and touched the tissue to the baby's head. "Nicole, I baptize you in the name of the Father, and of the Son, and of the Holy Spirit."

The chaplain said nothing else—the tears were more eloquent than any words (John Pattan, *Ministry to Theology*).

DISCO

This is the Latin word for "I learn." "Disciple," therefore, means "learner" more than "follower."

Learning can be a joy and so can teaching. When they come together, knowledge happens. But the teacher needs to be willing to see what the pupil does not, and be willing to take all the time the pupil needs to develop curiosity about what is not understood. Thus, the good teacher influences the student to be his/her own teacher. The educated know what they do not know—the ignorant do not.

This day's reading has two of John Baptist's disciples curious about Jesus, and so he asks them, "What are you looking for?" They obviously want more than a casual chat with him, so they invite themselves to lunch—a long one— till four P.M., "Teacher, where are you staying?" Good teacher that Jesus was, he answers, "Come and see." Find out for yourselves!

A pedagogue with all the answers is probably not asking the right questions. Truth is as illusive as is the luxury of certainty. Quick-fix conclusions only promote dependency on the answer-man. The most useful schools and churches are not filling stations where enlightenment is pumped in passively, but where doubt and dissent are not dismissed, but confronted courteously and discussed. "Any authentic community is founded on participation. Its structure is correct only if it admits the practical effectiveness of opposition." Karol Wojtyla said that in 1970. He was Pope John Paul II in 1978.

Ideas need bodies to live in, and that is why "the Word became flesh." Education is sensory as well as cerebral; a collaboration of the concrete with the abstract. Live experiencing reduces unreal theorizing. Students can sometimes learn as much from the class picnic as in the classroom. So Jesus gathered a group around him, as was the custom for master educators of that time.

And what a group it was—a doubter, a denier, a betrayer! In this first Christian seminary class there were three sets of brothers: Andrew and Simon Peter; James and John; and James the Less (meaning younger) and Jude Thaddeus, cousins of Jesus. Andrew seemed to be a good middleman, introducing his brother to the Lord; the youngster with the box lunch of five loaves and two fishes; and some foreigner Greeks who wanted to meet Jesus. Simon Peter was named "Satan" one time by the irked Jesus (Matthew 57: 13). James and John were regarded as aggressive enough to be nicknamed "Sons of Thunder." There is virtually no press on the other two brothers. Then there was Twin Thomas; guileless Bartholomew (John 1: 47); Philip, the quisling tax collector; Matthew; Simon, the terrorist; and the tragic Judas Iscariot, a suicide and the only nonlocal of the dozen. The press, reporting the scandalous behavior of current clergy, would find ample copy in this handpicked collection. Still, they were the apostles of the Good News who Jesus personally selected. As candidates for the ministry today, few of them would probably pass inspection. God does not need moral heavyweights to get His job done!

Despite his magnetic attraction, Jesus must have been a puzzle to these men. He did not resemble a prophet as did the Baptist. He was not an austere ascetic. He liked parties and did not mind dining with the riffraff. To the law and order set, Jesus was a nonviolent provocateur . . . except for the time he threw the furniture around in the Temple (Mark

11: 15). For the moral majority, he was too laid-back. To the silent minority, he was too noisy. Jesus was an outsider—unconventional—but he must have been a gifted leader to hold those disparate personalities together. Undoubtedly he was a good teacher; patient with questions, acceptant of diversity, tolerant for however long it took to get his message. By his civil demeanor he taught that arguments fail when issues are met instead of people. He wanted his disciples to be more on their toes than on their knees. He allowed them to verify for themselves that the reality experience is something one gets just after one needs it.

We learn most from people who are different from us, and from teachers who give us roots and wings.

21

LET FREEDOM WRING

This chapter reflects a smattering of all three of today's readings. The first features the Archie Bunker of the Old Testament—the reluctant prophet, Jonah. Typical of bigots, he is narrow-minded, self-righteous and preoccupied with his own comfort. Reneging on his preaching assignment to the Hebrew's cruelest enemy, the hated Ninevites (present day Iran), he almost kills himself playing it safe in escape. A fearful storm erupts at sea; Jonah's shifty behavior gives him away. The frightened mariners finger him as the reason for their perilous ill fortune and make him walk the plank. In this preposterous story, even the whale that swallows Jonah won't have him. Regurgitated onto dry land, Jonah concludes that he better take the Ninevites job seriously. Surprise, surprise! The detested antagonists get converted, to Jonah's acute chagrin. He is a very sore winner! He is about as happy at this unexpected turn of events, as would be Archie when he publicly, piously denounces a gay-lesbian rally and they turn about and march to the church he attends.

Oliver Wendell Holmes said: "The mind of a bigot is like the pupil of the eye. The more light poured on it, the more it will contract."

The bigot resents the light that binds. He has low tolerance for diversity. He needs an enemy to feel one-up-on. He does not understand that superiority is the obsession of inferiority. To play one-up, he is unaware that he has to be one-down.

What the bigot is down-on he is not up-on, so he belittles. The inevitable consequence is being little! The Jonah story points out that God even uses bigots for His merciful purpose.

In the second reading, Paul, like many millennialists, did not expect the world to be around much longer. His urge to detach from the "things of this world," including husbands from their wives, is a bit hard to take, unless he is insisting that a line needs to be drawn between self and possessions, if possessions are not to be possessors. Still, Paul knew the value of human beings. Things were to be sensibly used, and people dearly cherished. He understood how one can find oneself by being lost in another. He discovered this in his relationship with Christ. Married couples find this in one another; I doubt if God finds this as unfair competition for His affection.

In the third reading, Mark has the celebrated Baptist in jail. The stage is now set for Jesus and for his opening on the road, Galilee. This is a lakeside province of Northern Israel. Fish is its principal industry and Jesus begins collecting his apostles among its work force. Their response to his call is unhesitating. Impulsive, perhaps—risky for sure—but the adventure that lay ahead of them beats any small town fishing career.

Decisiveness is the mark of a winner. Annie Dillard is a contemporary animated author who illuminates this characteristic in her autobiography, *An American Childhood*. Annie enjoyed playing football with the boys. Her dad gave her some sound advice about tackling: "You've got to throw yourself *mightily* at the runner's legs." Injury more likely results from half-hearted, timid attempts. The lamb who takes on the lion should not be surprised at the outcome. But the lamb willing to stake all has the heart of a lion.

To fling oneself into what one decides to do—the job, a cause, a relationship—is surprisingly invigorating. There are no bad decisions. There is always learning, since good judgment comes from bad judgment. Life may wring us dry, still the Good News insists there is "another life," but it is in this one.

RELIGION VS. SPIRITUALITY

Though tradition bills him as a carpenter, the Gospels make no mention of Jesus ever having done work. They record him only as an itinerant preacher—and a good one. His audition at the synagogue of Capernaum earned a rave review. "The people were astonished at his teaching, for he taught them as one having authority and not as the scribes.... His fame spread everywhere throughout the whole region of Galilee." Jesus was a hit!

Now, who were "the scribes?" They were a professional class of trained copyists, notaries. Duplication of the written Hebrew scriptures gained them regard for being learned in the Law of Moses. From their group, Pharisees (*Peru shim*, derived from the Hebrew word meaning "separated") were recruited. They were notorious for their obsession with the literal practice of the Law in its minute details. This is what happens when a religion becomes a book!

There is no record of written Hebrew until about 1,000 B.C. Around the reign of King David, Jewish oral tradition of the preceding millennium was collected to form the first books of the Bible. Books have lives of their own. Especially important books. They spawn analysts, specialists who assert particular insights about what the books mean. The scribes (*sopherim*, in Hebrew) apparently assumed this claim, but they were dull, as legal wranglers often are. The briefs of Supreme Court judges on a constitutional fine point would hardly storm bestseller heaven!

Jesus was not dull. He wowed the audience according to Mark. What did he say that so stunned them? We only know that he said it with *authority*. He was authentic. Authenticity inevitably commands attention any time the speaker's source is the depths of his inner self rather than the theories from other authorities.

To believe in oneself takes being in touch with that self—all the parts of the self—the glad, the sad, the mad, and the bad. Once acknowledged; and without judgment, one can begin to be centered, to assimilate events rather than be crushed by them. This availability to reality produces a rare security. Jesus seemed to have this assurance. He had come to know himself. His inner struggles are metaphorically dramatized in the Gospel account of his desert temptations. Intimacy with his own feelings and ideas opened his sensitivity to life about him. Self-aware, he could be perceptive of others. That's his *authority*! He was outside what he was inside. Jesus was *transparent*, according to theologian Paul Tillich (1886-1965).

This quality does not come from study, or deliberate intent, or intense religion. It is an unmerited gift of grace— a spirituality that recognizes the awesome sacredness of life. It believes in a Creator that believes in His creatures, who sees them as partners in His nonstop creating process, and not the subordinates of an Almighty Egoist demanding to be pleased.

Jesus knew about the human heart because he knew something about the hungers of his own. He knew rules and ritual were not food enough. The serenity he experienced with his Father was the Good News he wanted the world to be in on.

By-the-book religion attracts the structure-hungry; uneasy with inquiry, they tend to settle for the quick-fix theology of cliché evangelists. They are forever taking their morality temperatures and righteously consign the unchurched to the *pit*.

Spirituality brings a lighter touch to the life of faith. Its attention is on the light, not the road map. The light is the path. Spirituality knows that the universe is in Good Hands, so it can be tranquil about the uncertainties, the ambiguities of existence. The paradoxical ambivalence of the human condition elicits sympathy rather than censure.

In the late '80s a memorable TV series, *The Power of Myth*, featured Bill Moyers interviewing Professor Joseph Campbell, the renowned master of the meaning of mythology. In one of the sequences, Campbell offered his view of the difference between religion and spirituality.

I had a friend who attended an international meeting of Roman Catholic meditative orders, which was held in Bangkok. He told me that the Catholic monks had no problems understanding the Buddhist monks, but that it was the clergy of the two religions who were unable to understand each other. The person who had a mystical experience knows that all the symbolic expressions of it are faulty. The symbols do not render the experiences, they suggest it. If you haven't had the experience, how can you know what it is? (*The Power of Myth*, p. 60)

The scribes expounded on the external symbols of their religion—i.e. "the label on the bottle." Jesus let the people taste the wine.

5th Sunday of Ordinary Time
(Job 7: 1-7, 1 Corinthians 9: 16-23, Mark 1: 29-39)

MISSION IMPASSABLE

Like the man says, no one makes it out of this life either tearless or alive. All three of this day's readings draw attention to the mystery of our mortal travail. Mark, ever in a hurry, records a busy day for Jesus. Most likely disturbed by the suffering surrounding him, sleep eludes Jesus. Rising before light, he seeks solace in prayer and solitude. But no rest for the weary! He is pursued: "Everyone is looking for you." He meets the demand. George Bernard Shaw (1856-1950) applauds this response:

> This is the true joy of life, the being used for a purpose recognized by yourself as a mighty one: the being thoroughly worn out before you are thrown on the scrap heap: being a force of Nature instead of a feverish, selfish little clod of ailments and grievances, complaining that the world will not devote itself to making you happy.

Why should the world owe anything to anybody? It was here first!

Paul tries adjusting to his mission by "being all things to all men"—a ready recipe for burnout. However, the Pauline effort may have been less motivated to patronize or to people-please, than to defer his vigorous opinions to others equally opinionated. Boswell (1740-1795) praises Dr. Samuel Johnson (1709-1784) for his "readiness to throw himself into the interest of other people." Such gracious accommodating is to "walk in another's moccasins." An

31

underrated social virtue—this willingness to see another point of view.

Now for the masterpiece—the matchless ancient folk tale—Job! Composed about five centuries before Christ, it is considered to be the longest surviving Hebrew poem. Superbly written, it is a bold tale about divine atrocity; the bad things that happen to a good man.

The drama opens with God conducting a staff meeting with His celestial cabinet, of which Satan (Hebrew for "prosecuting attorney") is a member. The Deity gets hooked into a crooked wager with Satan. They bet on a perfectly honorable dupe named Job: the former, playing Job to win; the latter, to lose. An avalanche of horrors befall Job to test his fidelity to God and to virtue. His faith holds: "We accept good things from God—ought we not accept bad?"

The narrative describes Job as so foul smelling from his assorted diseases, that he is deposited on the top of a (bleep) pile. His agonies are augmented by the annoying advice of insipid friends. His soured spouse urges him to "curse God and die." Still Job persists in his innocence and angrily stands up to an indifferent God: "I will defend my ways to His face. I hold fast my righteousness, I will not let go."

Job respects God enough to confront Him candidly. Exasperated, he pleads "why?" God's answer is no answer, but a snooty-sounding put-down for impugned divine sovereignty. Job is stumped—told off. There is little left to do but accept. A change takes place. Bitterness softens to discernment. A bigger picture comes into focus, reducing his self-pity and resentment. No longer a victim, Job forgives God. In fact, Job comes off looking better than God.

Job personifies a quality dear to the Jewish heart—*chutzpah*, a Yiddish term for audacity, gall, nerve, "guts." God apparently endorses this by restoring Job to even more abundance than before. The legend does not resolve the mystery of why the innocent suffer. Rabbi Kushner, in his celebrated bestseller, *When Bad Things Happen To Good People*, suggests that a more useful question than "Why?" is, "What can I do when disaster strikes?" Job's troubles occasioned the discovery of unknown resources in himself.

The Job story is fiction. The Anne Frank story is fact. The famous *Diary of Anne Frank* recounts this remarkable child's ordeals under the Nazis. A holocaust victim, this bright-eyed smiling youngster showed the world how to stay human in an inhuman existence. She died in the Bergen Belsen death camp just days before its liberation. Her last recorded thought: "In spite of everything I still believe that people are good at heart."

That tops chutzpah!

FAMILIARITY THAT BREEDS CONTENT

If you have ever felt anonymous, abandoned, like a nonperson, you had a feeble hint of what it was like to be a leper in days of yore. Cruelly quarantined from all family and friends, they were forbidden all human interaction. Often repulsively disfigured, they were piously scorned as outcasts by an angry God brutally punishing them for their sins. Their isolation was living death.

Any skin blemish was considered leprosy in those days. That meant that psoriasis, dermatitis, ringworm, even measles or chicken pox, were treated as a leprous plague. Since there was no knowledge that bacteria cause infectious diseases, demon possession was blamed, and priests were put in charge of public health.

Most of us have experienced, at one time or other, the castaway sensation . . . as a child, to be second banana to a preferred sibling. Later, to be passed over for promotion after twenty loyal years while a young hotshot, only six months with the firm, gets your coveted prize. Or to be downsized out after thirty grinding years, and now you are over 55! Or you raised the four kids, supported him to his M.D., and now he wants out for that cute nurse! Why? It's not fair!

Somehow you got through it. You survived. Some even got a better deal. Valentine's Day is the day to celebrate that living "good deal" in our separate lives, that unexpected "break" we could not imagine that we deserved. Valentine's Day merits more liturgical prominence than the Church accords it. Maybe it should be a Holy Day of Obligation like Immaculate Conception or All Saints. What other feast day acknowledges more of what the human heart is all about: the need for and the gift of intimate human caring? If you have been rescued from isolation by someone who stopped long enough to notice you—to want to share, to mutually disclose—you know the miracle that set you on the road to wholeness. You have a valentine!

Thirty-five years ago I ensconced my aging parents in a senior citizen community that happily suited their declining years. They have since passed on and now I live where they lived. I do not find it exciting. The mean age of the residents is 75. There are no children to enliven the stillness. But one feature never fails to move me—the sight of an elderly couple taking their daily walk together hand-in-hand.

As a celibate, I muse to myself about them. . . . All the years of talking together, thinking together, worrying together, the differing, the arguing, the disappointments. I ponder the innumerable forgivenesses, the "I'm sorry"s, the "I didn't mean it"s. There is no place to hide from the full-length mirror that each one is to the other. There can be no hit and run when they promised each other to see it through. They have something durable now. Relationships change, commitments do not. They fell in love many years ago and they have come to know how to stand up straight in it. It was never easy.

Learning to live together yielded a liberating side effect: outliving the narcissism that every infant is born with. People who need people and have what they need, are never bored. There never is nothing to do. There is always something to do for the other. What a break to have something more than oneself to live for! May all you sweethearts continue to enjoy each other as God surely enjoys His "funny valentines."

THROUGH THE ROOF

Tired from an extended tour of Galilean synagogues, Jesus returns to Capernaum, his chosen home, for a breather and a standing-room-only audience. Mark depicts a scene worthy of the Marx Brothers. While lecturing to a full house, four fellows are tearing up the roof over his head in order to get a paralyzed friend within healing touch of Jesus. What would you do if some strangers were scuttling your roof? I would call the cops, or at least 911! Jesus looks up and he sees faith. He sees marvelous, single-minded, enterprising caring for a helpless friend. He probably smiled as he said to the paralytic, "Child, your sins are forgiven."

For the assembled scribes, the self-appointed assessors of religious orthodoxy, that declaration was too much. "Who does he think he is . . . God? Blasphemy!" Why did Jesus risk agitating these rigid certifiers? Obviously he wished to make a point. He wanted to disabuse people of thinking of God as a hanging judge poised to sentence the wayward with savage penalties simply for being human. In those days, Judaism indissolubly linked sin to sickness. Disease and suffering were God's judgment for sins. Jesus wished to refute sin and suffering as cause and effect. But how could he subvert a venerable religious mindset and not offend the tradition experts? Getting into an argument about it—the "I'm right, you're wrong" approach—would be futile. So, Jesus meets the opposition on their own ground. Using their logic, he reasons, "If sin is the cause of this paralysis, then if the paralysis is removed, so is the sin." God is no longer the heavy!

Arguing fails when questions are answered instead of questioners. Knowing their fondness for debating fine points of the Law, Jesus addresses this puzzling poser to the scribes: "Which is easier to say to the paralytic: 'your sins are forgiven,' or 'rise up, pick up your mat and walk'?"

Why this strange query? Could Jesus be implying that to forgive and to do a miracle are the same thing? That one is just as difficult to perform as the other, but both are within human power? Might he be intimating that in God's eyes, to forgive is the miracle cure for the human condition? That the healing in forgiveness gives life back to the forgiven as well as the forgiver? Still, forgiveness is not possible unless the forgiver sees in himself that same capacity for evil he so loathes in the enemy.

This gospel could be making another salient point, namely, that pain is not God's penalty, but God's opportunity. What can deepen, teach, mellow, and strengthen the soul more than suffering endured? The memory of crosses and crises survived provides our most confident personal self-image. Thus, no lifetime is spared them.

That is why Jesus wanted his church to be a sanctuary for the world's rejects: gays, addicts, divorced, criminals, religious derelicts. He wanted it to be the defender, not the accuser of mankind. He wanted his church to be a mystical presence of compassion, hospitable to dissent, gracious to antagonists. He did not need it to be an institutional power broker—a closed corporation of efficiency exclusively reserved for the elect. He wanted his church to be a servant church, but bold enough to go through the roof for us spiritual cripples.

WE THERE YET?

In this Gospel I hear Jesus designate what is important to him about life and religion. To him, life and religion are one piece. Worshipping God and making a living are equally urgent. To his scandalized critics, he obviously preferred feasting to fasting and seemed quite comfortable doing the former with the local riff-raff. Who could better benefit? The point is clear that fellowship with Jesus did not exclude moral derelicts who enjoyed his company. In a subsequent age, any church operating in his name would therefore need the welcome mat out for those whom a righteous society looked down its nose at. Might that mean the Mafia, crooked cops, druggies, gays, and streetwalkers? Seems so! The sick are the charges of the hospital, just as the church is a sanctuary for the disreputable.

Relating to his Father was upbeat for Jesus. He consistently identified the kingdom of God—that is, when goodness takes over—as a party. He even styles himself as the bridegroom at a wedding feast who wants his guests to have a good time. With Lent just around the corner, the liturgy cheerfully emphasizes festal nuptial imagery. Fasting is associated with the rites of mourning. Sadly, there is a time for that. But Jesus insinuates that grimness must not distinguish the face of his disciples.

Where did the Church pick up that God somehow is pleased with human corporal austerity? How does severe monastic asceticism bring God nearer? What possessed the buoyant St. Francis of Assisi, so jubilantly relishing the glories of nature, to so cruelly punish his body in the name of the love of God? He apparently repented when he confessed to his worn form at his premature demise, "I have not been very kind to you, have I, Brother Ass?" Jesus may have felt that life was tough enough on people without religion imposing further hardship.

Jesus, therefore, brought a new look to the mien of religion. Solemn was not necessarily sacred. As the environs of Paradise were approached, the epic poet Dante distinguished the sound of the celestial music of the sphere to be laughter. When visiting San Francisco, Mother Teresa was asked by a sober young woman, "What must I do to be a saint?" The holy nun's one-word response: "Smile!"

This lighthearted focus was the Good News of Jesus. He referred to it as "new wine"; new wine that would shatter the shrunken wineskins of weary ritual that routine repetition had rendered stale. In fact, the occupational hazard of organized religion is the illusion that tradition is holy just because it is old. Spontaneity, freshness, and flexibility react to the "now," not the "then." Small wonder that this luminous insight is such a contemporary hit: "The past is history, the future is mystery, that is why the gift of 'now' is called the present."

Old sacrosanct habits die hard. Jesus obviously was sensitive to the incompatibility of the old being imposed upon the new. Applying an old shrinkable patch to a new shrink-resistant fabric made as much sense as medically prescribing former bloodletting to cure modern pneumonia. Still, he pressed his avant-garde message that valued service to human needs over obsessive devotional practices. God does not need the attention that people need, and he knew how difficult change could be. Mark Twain once remarked that the only one that enjoys it is "a wet baby."

For Jesus, living was not a tidy lockstep march to a regimented cadence. It is a journey through a minefield of unforeseen vicissitudes. The pilgrimage on the way back to the Author of Life is a zigzag course of constant adjustment to the unfamiliar. Jesus saw himself as supplying the mature spirituality that this odyssey demands when he promised, "I have come to give you more abundant life"—not more religion (John 10: 10). Are we there yet? Almost! That is when you live life lightly, connect with everything, but belong to yourself.

THE LITTER OF THE LAW

If you have visited New York City, you probably visited St. Patrick's Cathedral on Fifth Avenue. It is an uncommon experience to step from the flurry of the noisy Manhattan street into the soft tranquillity of that splendid church. Despite its stately interior, it has the feel of a quiet village wayside chapel. The sense of God is palpable.

The ancient Hebrews invented the Sabbath to enjoy this unruffled serenity within the bustle of a busy week. It was intended to be a rest from daily toil, a one-day holiday of relaxation with the family, an unhurried communion with the Lord. The lowliest drudge was entitled to this blessed interlude of ease and thanksgiving.

How could this regenerative holy rite so twist into becoming a trap of petty prohibitions and repressive restrictions? Lighting a candle, brushing your teeth, combing your hair were proscribed as forbidden labor by the religious authorities. I recall as a boy, the reward of a chocolate from the local synagogue sexton for simply snapping on the lights each Saturday morning. . . . How can such oppressive legalisms become accepted devotional practice? What pervades the psyche of religious leadership that needs to manage its votaries' behavior in such stifling detail? Controlling people can be a heady enterprise, and the clergy are not above this intoxication, especially when justified as enforcing "God's law." The will to power is a natural human impulse, but it's particularly the preoccupation of the impotent.

I remember a psychology class in the '70s conducted by Rollo May, himself an ordained minister. His impression of the cloth: "The clergy reflect two main characteristics for me," he said. "One is positive, the other negative. The positive one is the earnest desire to help people. The negative one is the divine right to be taken care of."

Less than omnipotent, our deplored human dependencies can promote unconscious defenses, such as insensitive authoritarian governance over others. That is why Jesus cut through the legalistic detritus of the rabbinical code by declaring, "The Sabbath was made for man, not man for the Sabbath."

This pithy wisdom is not saying that religious institutions, rituals, rules, dogmas and spiritual discipline are not important. It is saying that they are not sacred; human beings are. If this logic is valid, then the hallowed foundations in our lives—church, school, court of law, marriage, the nation—never preempt the human person in value. They are meant to serve people, not vice versa.

In tune with this theme, how might Lent, commencing again on Wednesday, best serve our individual humanity? What do each of us need more of for fuller living . . . time with family, exercise, reading? What can we use less of . . . tobacco, TV, alcohol, snacking between meals? This Lent is our big chance to go for our best selves.

Another Lenten suggestion: pick out one person you feel needs you most. Invest in that person, focus, listen, relate, take your time, get acquainted. You may decide that one person is your very self. Then let this Lent make you your own best friend. This is not easy, knowing yourself as you do. No mortification is more difficult or more worthwhile. Getting to know you is the surest way of getting to like you. You deserve it—go for it!

CHOICE VS. CHANCE

Yes, there probably was a deluge; floods were quite common in the Euphrates Valley. No, Joan of Arc was not Noah's wife! A recent poll reported that ten percent of Bible readers thought she was. Like life, the Bible is not easy to understand. It is called the Word of God, and it seems to be not so much the word of God about God, as much as the word of God about mankind. In his potent little 1999 volume, *The Heart Is A Little To The Left*, William Sloane Coffin comments:

> I read the Bible because the Bible reads me. I see myself reflected in Adam's excuses, in Saul's envy of David, in promise-making, promise-breaking Peter. . . . I find a God who not only answers our questions, but equally importantly, questions our answers. . . . If you take the Bible seriously, you can't take it literally—not all of it.

The Bible is a Jewish book. Both Old and New Testaments were written by Jews, for Jews. It is the Hebrew attempt to figure out God. That is why it reflects so many varied faces of divinity: a militant monarch, a tender shepherd, a testy sovereign insisting on unquestioning obeisance, as well as a playful Creator enjoying His creatures. These are all projections of the Hebrew mind trying to make sense of their God experience in their phenomenal history. Scholars date the beginnings of the written scriptures at about 750 centuries before Christ. Preceding this was the oral tradition—campfire stories retold from generation to generation. The first five books, the Pentateuch, were probably put together about five centuries before Christ. Incidents related in Genesis, like the Garden of Eden story and the Tower of Babel, can be found in Sumerian/Babylonian folktales as far back as three millennia before Christ. The Flood story is one of these.

The sacred writers consistently sought the Deity's personal involvement in Hebrew history and thus interpolated the Divine Presence in their major fortunes. Calamity meant God's displeasure; prosperity, His approbation. Their writing is about religious experience, not a factual chronicle. So, what's the point of the Noah story? That God has feelings much like themselves: truculent, rueful, contrite? The legend reveals the Creator admitting a mistake when He created humans, and deciding to clean out the mess with a Deluge and start over. Like a sensitive parent who deplores overpunishing a child, God regrets His harshness and makes a rainbow as a promise that He means business about forgiveness. The story affirms that a "process God" can change His mind.

In the typical hurry-up style of Mark, this Gospel reading features a condensed version of Jesus' desert temptations. He apparently resolved any dilemma about the nature of God when he referred to Him as "Father." He may not have been that sure about himself, however. He knew he had to go public with this message. How should he present it? Who should he be: celebrity, CEO, commandant? Or just take his chances being vulnerable? It is the typical struggle of identity for anyone embarking on a career. What will assist success—people pleasing, assertiveness, or just being teachable? This vexing introspection, for anyone open to daily experience and to growth, endures longer than forty days!

According to Matthew's fuller account, Jesus resorted to citing Bible principles to guide his path of action. Clearly his traditional religious background offered the advantage of controlling his deliberate choice over random chance or impulsive instinct. Parents who deny their children religious training in the name of sparing them "brainwashing" or "guilt indoctrination," sadly set them on life's sea in a rudderless vessel. Guilt is not irrevocable injury if it prompts amendment for the harm done, or forestalls the harm planned. An unfortunate death row inmate lamented, "I always had choices in my life, but I was never taught to consider consequences."

A cartoon depicts two elderly nuns chatting together. One says to the other, "This is a letter from a former pupil. She says she forgives me for ruining her life." The capacity to forgive sounds like a healthy consequence!

PLUCK OF THE IRISH

Among my varied handicaps, one of them is not being Irish. Just hearing brogue, I'm on the floor! Though I boast no relic of Erin in my middle-European heritage, I cannot think of the transfiguration and not think of Ireland. The incandescent divinity that shone on Mt. Tabor was soon followed by the hideous Crucifixion on Mt. Calvary. The flame of glowing faith ignited by St. Patrick did not exempt the Irish from their centuries of agony.

In his splendid book, *How the Irish Saved Civilization*, Thomas Cahill describes early fifth century Ireland as a brooding, dank island whose inhabitants, while externally carefree and warlike, lived with quaking fear within. Their terror of shape-changing monsters, of sudden death and the insubstantiality of their world was so acute that they drank themselves into an insensate stupor in order to sleep. Patrick provided a welcome alternative. The Christianity he proposed to the Irish succeeded because it removed the dread of the magical world that haunted them. Once Christianized, they enriched civilization with the monastic movement and the laborious copying of valuable books otherwise lost to history.

Nonetheless, the sad threnody of the Irish story laments centuries of British cruelty; the potato blight and famine of 1840; a century-long recession; an uprooting emigration. By 1870, thirty-three percent of the foreign born in the U.S.A. were Irish and painfully unwelcome. "Irish Need Not Apply" greeted their employment efforts. Back home, there was the bloody civil war for Irish independence

(1918-1921) and the continued strife currently between Northern Ulster and Southern Eire.

The poet William Butler Yeats (1865 -1939) sums up the Irishman's soul: "Being Irish he had an abiding sense of tragedy which sustained him through temporary periods of joy."

Still no misery has disfigured that soul. However victimized, they would not surrender to victimhood. Whatever their travail, they refused to cry the "blues." The Irish are simply not a "poor me" society. They have a knack for making a song, a story, a jest of their heartache. In fact, they are transfigured by their troubles. The world rejoices in the mirth and mayhem the Irish have brought to the staid Anglo Saxon culture. How about this twist? "To those who love us—love us. For those who don't—may God turn them. If He can't turn them, may He turn their ankles . . . So we may know them by their limp."

Then there was Bridget O'Malley repairing to Father Grady in tears:

"Ah, Bridget, what can be so wrong as to upset you so?"

"Oh, Father, I've got terrible news. Me husband died last night!"

"God save us," replied the priest. "Tell me, Bridget, did he make any last requests?"

"That he did, Father. Mr. O'Malley asked me, 'Bridget, for God's sake, put down that gun!'"

(Thanks to Father Bill O'Donnell for the above goodies!)

One more time . . .

Paddy is on trial for robbery. For lack of evidence, the judge acquits him. Paddy then says to the judge, "Does that mean I can keep the money?"

So, on this feast of Transfiguration, I raise my Guinness to the nation of saints and scholars. Though I have nary a teardrop of Hibernian blood in me, I feel singularly blessed with a share of their Gaelic wit and whimsy.

Erin Go Bragh!

REAL ZEAL

Those turned off by the effete-looking holy card Jesus can have a ball with this Gospel. Gentle Jesus—meek and mild—is throwing the Temple furniture around. "He made a whip out of cords . . . spilled the coins of the money changers and overturned their tables." Why this out-of-control violence from the one who urged turning the other cheek, walking the extra mile, giving your shirt away, and loving one's enemies? A hint is offered as "his disciples recalled the words of scripture: 'zeal for your house will consume me.'"

Jesus was not the first religious teacher to denounce the crass commercialism in the great Temple. The prophets, Jeremiah, Zachariah, and Malachi, all warned that God could not be trapped by codes of ceremonial observance. God was better served by solicitude for one another than by ritual procedures. But Jesus was the first to put his actual muscle into his words. Surely he must have known that this eruption would hardly change things. There was probably business as usual the next day. After all, Temple money exchange was sanctioned by the highest religious authority, since Roman coins were forbidden in Temple transactions. The Talmud prescribed a one-half *shekel* tax (almost two days' wage) as an allowed fee for the money changer. Fleecing impoverished pilgrims by exorbitant rates infuriated Jesus.

He also may have felt that it was high time to make a strong statement on the irrelevance of animal sacrifice.

Seven centuries before, Isaiah (1: 11-17) declared God's scorn for the bloody custom:

> "What to me is the multitude of your sacri-fices?" says the Lord! "I have had enough of burnt offerings of rams and the fat of fed beasts; I do not delight in the blood of bulls, or of lambs, or of goats. Bring no more vain offerings."

His vehement action announces vividly that heaven is not embezzled by money, nor is God domesticated by ritual.

Jesus was as out of line as the Selma marchers or the jailed protesters of abortion clinics and capital punishment. His startling performance sends the clear clarion call that there are some things we should not stand for; outrages that should outrage human beings . . . such as extravagant defense spending when schools need to be built, or obscene campaign expenditures, or foot-dragging on gun control legislation.

Jesus' white-hot wrath helps clarify confusion about the validity of intense emotions. True, anger can be dangerous. So can food, sun, and water. But emotions are innocent in themselves. Like children, they need to be heard, attended to, if they are to be controlled. Aggressive feelings are often uncomfortable and embarrassing, so the natural tendency is to shove them under the rug. Anger denied can build to volcanic fury. This is the case with many a serial killer, whose neighbors report him as "never any trouble, just kept to himself." Anger needs advertence. When recognized and dealt with, it can be a dynamic advantage to vital living.

One expedient formula for handling upsetting emotion is "Name it-Claim it-Aim it." That is, label the feeling consciously for what it is: annoyance, hurt, or rage. Then, own it as one's own without blaming another for it. Finally, direct what is felt to the offender simply by saying, "I am hurt/uneasy/furious," not, "you make me mad!"

Anger is a perfectly respectable emotion. In the face of threat, it is far more serviceable than terror. Even the Bible refers to the "wrath of God." This is another way of saying that, unlike Rhett Butler in *Gone with the Wind*, God "gives a damn" about human behavior. We are important to Him. Therefore, anger has something to do with caring. The opposite of love is not hate or anger, it is *indifference*. We are generally angered only by what is important to us. Psychology claims that the other face of anger is fear. One might usefully ask oneself when angry: "What am I afraid of?" It could be the threat of losing something precious.

Passion is a bounteous gift in anyone's life. The late, great Paddy Chayefsky conceives the Creator's evaluation on this subject in his luminous play *Gideon*.

> It is Passion, Gideon, that carries man to God. And passion is a balky beast. Few men ever let it out of the stable. It brooks no bridle; indeed, it bridles you; it rides the rider. Yet, it inspirits man's sessile soul above his own inadequate world and makes real such things as beauty, fancy, love and God and all those other things that are not quite molecular but are. Passion is the very fact of God in man that makes him other than a brute.

Our human brain weighs about three pounds and consists of one hundred billion cells, of which, we are told, we use only ten percent. However, this tiny corporeal computer surpasses the one hundred million galaxies surrounding us, because it can think, get exasperated, and love!

LA VIE EN ROSE

Today is the Sunday of the Rose. In contrast to the somber season of purple, the liturgy injects this flash of color to remind earnest worshippers that lighthearted is as holy as solemn—perhaps more so. It used to be called *Laetare* (Latin imperative for "rejoice") Sunday. In its commanding way, the Church is commending balance to its disciplined followers.

The first reading (2 Chron. 36: 14-23) catches no euphoria of the day. "The anger of the Lord against His people was so inflamed." But it closes on the cheery note as Persian King Cyrus repatriates the exiled Jews to their homeland. The second reading (2 Eph. 2: 4-10) comes closer to the keynote as Paul exults in "the immeasurable riches of His grace in His kindness to us in Christ Jesus."

The Gospel is hard to follow. Jesus sounds more like an abstruse academic lecturing a dull student. His words are abstract, stilted, unlike the homespun plain-talk in the synoptic versions. The generations subsequent to his death were better able to evaluate the impact of that Risen Life in the lives of his followers, much as later generations can more clearly comprehend the significance of deceased presidents and their influence on world and national history. John's Gospel was put together about the end of the first century and reflects a developed Christology. It could be that the author affirmed the divinity of Jesus as a fit competitor for the homage the self-proclaimed *divine* Caesars demanded. Matthew, Mark and Luke do not highlight Jesus as God.

The Nicodemus nocturnal visitation is the same as our story when "what will people think" rules our behavior. Nicodemus was a prominent citizen, a respected religious leader. He was not about to expose his reputation to any suspicion by a detected involvement with the upstart Nazarene. To court public approval usually means abdicating a part of oneself. A performer who depends on the audience to define him will never win an Oscar. The consummate actor is always more convincing when he plays his role as he sees it.

Nicodemus was not sure where he stood. He was stuck with the old time religion: rules, ritual, a God insisting on strict ceremonial observance. Jesus saw religion principally as duty to people and less as devotion to external structure. Nicodemus must have liked what he heard. But it may have been strange sounding to him, possibly far-out, certainly unconventional. Then there was possibly that nagging anxiety about disloyalty to a revered tradition. So, Nicodemus was cautious, if not timid, about endorsing openly the controversial young teacher. Still, to his credit, he made a move. However nervous, it was a baby step out of the dark.

Jesus rewarded this circumspect gesture with an enigmatic response. He was sensitive to the human resistance to change, but he emphasized that there was no growth without it. "Unless you are born again," he states, "you can never get into the Kingdom of God." Another simpler translation of this text: "You must be reborn from above." What does this mean? It mystified Nicodemus as well. One interpretation could be that personal education involves forgetting much of what was learned in the past. Grownups discover eventually that what got them through childhood does not work as well in adulthood. Cooing, cajoling, crying, and tantrums may have been effective once; now mature relating is called for. Jesus' focus on reverence for human beings is as good a lesson to learn as even the most scholarly erudition. Those gifted with this modest understanding have discovered that gentleness is an amazingly durable attribute and its offspring is joy. Want joy in your life? Try a little tenderness!

NEVER SAY DIE . . . !

John's Gospel features Jesus in conversation more than in action. It is thus more abstract and prolix, as theological thinking often is. The death of Lazarus provides the occasion for Jesus to advance his doctrine about mankind's most distressing destiny, the grave. He is touched to tears at this loved friend's passing. Only one other time do the scriptures report him weeping: over apathetic Jerusalem. Death disturbed Jesus, as it does us all!

This episode wraps up for John the public ministry of Jesus and supplies a bridge to the story of his final days. Jesus senses the approaching end and talks about dying as the opportunity for a new and fuller life. He points to nature's rhythm as the buried seed produces a rich yield. "For nothing dies but something lives, till the skies be fugitives," so says the poet. Living and dying are of one piece for Jesus. Death is the entrance to real living; "eternal life" he calls it, for which all mankind was created. Earth's existence is only for openers. The best is yet to be!

Even science affirms this theology when it reasons that physical matter is indestructible. The tiny atom can be shattered, but in its diffusion, it becomes something else—energy. Base quantity is transformed into a higher form—activity. Incredible power is released from battered matter. So it is not so far-fetched to think of the human soul as immortal. To expire is to be transformed from a gross to a purer state—to pass to another time zone, another dimension.

This thinking may comfort the mourner, but it does not displace the aching emptiness that a loved one's loss creates in the griever's life. The deceased may be in a better place—the survivor is not. Why this wrenching agony? How does tragedy improve our lives? After standing tall, why must we be brought to our knees? Opposites seem to feed each other. Negative versus positive gives us electricity. Illness makes health precious. Not having makes having gladder. Suffering is inherent in the nature of mankind because it is imperfect, limited, and in process. Pain is an invitation to transcend, to reach beyond self. Compassion is born of it. When Jesus proclaimed, "Blessed are those who mourn," he was saying, fortunate are they who love enough to grieve.

Death, when it happens, we may no more be aware of than when we fall asleep. It's the dying that frightens us. How long will it take? Will it hurt? Will I trouble others? Will I be "chicken"? The final curtain may include all the above, but it is not the end of the play. It is only the intermission. Were it not for death, life would be an unrelenting soap opera without commercial breaks . . . a kind of perpetual insomnia. Dying takes practice—like letting go of Monday so it does not contaminate Tuesday. Kissing off the good and the bad of each day could well ease the shock of final departure.

Maybe dying is our last chance to get it right—our terminal choice for freedom. Have you noticed the serenity on the countenances of the demised? Worry, if you must, but the issue is in even better hands than Allstate! The popular Lutheran seminary professor, Joseph Sitler (born 1904), says it for me:

> The only life I know is this finite one that I live before dying. What life beyond might be, I have no notion. If all life is engendered and created by God, then that relationship will certainly not be destroyed by the periodic appearance and disappearance of

this particular person with my name. Something continues but what that will be I'm perfectly willing to leave in the hands of the Originator

—Grace Notes and Other Fragments
Joseph A. Sittler

KING FOR A DAY

The Romans reserved palm waving for their conquering emperors. The Jews brandished branches to commemorate the victorious entry of the warrior Maccabees into Jerusalem to rededicate the Temple. If the followers of Jesus wanted to display how much they thought of him, they did so at his own fatal expense. Ever sensitive to suspicions of sedition, any pretense of local prominence was viewed by the vigilant imperial occupation as politically incorrect. Five days later, Jesus was executed for the capital crime: being "King of the Jews," a claim he consistently and sedulously resisted.

Kingship never seemed to appeal to Jesus, but royalty did. Not the parliamentary variety, but the nobility of humility. Life, for most, is no walk in the park. Our planet is a perilous place. Awake or asleep danger lurks. Holy Week liturgy is a thicket of symbolism—an abridged reproduction of paradoxical human existence. The dramatic final days of Jesus offer insights about handling hurt.

The Passion narrative is remarkable for its simplicity— its matter-of-fact, emotionless recording of a gruesome horror. The stark event is reported like a telegram—without an extra syllable. Strange that the word *passion*, which signifies intensity, is not matched in its Gospel telling. In this Passion Play, we have played all the parts: Judas the betrayer, Peter the denier, Pilate the compromiser. There were times when we were the supporting cast: Mary and John beneath the cross, the merciful Veronica, whenever we attended the needs of a sufferer.

Some of us have known the desolation of "My God, my God, why have you forsaken me?" This soulful sob from tortured lips is the opening verse of Psalm 22. It does not end, however, on this forlorn note. Verse 24 revives hope: "For he has not despised my cries of despair; he has not turned and walked away. When I cried to him he heard me and came." This is faith speaking—the single most indispensable resource when disaster strikes. The temptation to repudiate faith is when we most need to believe—to believe that there is a plan, a purpose, a solution—that evil can never be the bottom line as long as there is a God.

To paraphrase the poet who understood something of the mystery of that Holy Week: Love means to love the unlovable, or it is not virtue at all. Forgiving means pardoning the unpardonable, or it is no virtue at all. Faith means believing the unbelievable, or it is no virtue at all. And hope means hoping in the hopeless, or it is no virtue at all.

Maybe this is what "royalty" means. It can happen to us without our even knowing that it is happening. It simply means playing the hand that life deals us. It often happens best when we feel least about our worth.

A reprise of Sister Mary Clare:

> Why did you make me, Lord,
> the way that I am,
> which is just as I would not
> wish to be?
> Did you perhaps know what You
> were about,
> And plan me thus for all
> eternity?

If I had fashioned me,
I would have used a sterner stuff,
and formed a soul more strong,
immune to pains of love
and deaf to tears,
unmoved by sentiment,
untouched by song!
But I, I am a fool; I feel too much,
At every little hurt,
I cringe and whine.
Did you intend that I
should win the cup by just
these handicaps of mine?

MINI-RESURRECTIONS

Headcounters report that more attend church for Easter than they do at Christmas. Why is this, do you suppose? Could be that as appealing as is the miracle of birth, rebirth is even more so. Spring says more about reanimation than does winter!

To elicit more consistent church attendance, a prankish pastor sported a touch of whimsy in his Easter sermon, by introducing a novel "No Excuse Sunday." He announced:

Cots will be placed in the foyer for those who say, "Sunday is my only day to sleep late." There will be a special section with lounge chairs and recliners for those who think our pews are too hard and uncomfortable. Eye drops will be available for those with tired eyes from the glare of late night Saturday TV programs. We will have steel helmets for those who say, "The roof would cave in if I ever came to church." Blankets will be furnished for those who think the church is too cold and drafty; fans will be given to those who say it is too hot and stuffy. Score cards will be distributed to those who wish to keep a record of the hypocrites present. Relatives and friends will be in attendance for those who can't go to church and cook dinner too. Ushers will pass around "Stamp Out Stewardship" buttons for those who are weary of being asked for money. One area of the church will be devoted to trees and grass for those who prefer to seek God in nature.

Doctors and nurses will be in attendance for those who plan to be sick on Sunday. We will provide hearing aids for those who can't hear the preacher and cotton for those who can. Hope to see you there. (*Celebration*, 23 April 2000)

People might be going to church for the wrong reason— to be inspired, when it is more useful to go to be inspirers. This is the wonder of the Paschal mystery—that we can be restorers of life to one another when we stop long enough to care.

Many of us have seen little resurrections . . . not stupendous, like bringing the dead to life, but seeing someone eased from the sepulcher of fear, of despair, of futile guilt. For many years, veterans' hospitals have ministered to the "walking wounded": men entombed in the memory of terror, afraid to move out to the scary land of other people . . . who seek peace in paralysis—emotional rigor mortis— too frightened to feel again. No amount of urging, badgering, or cheerleading could penetrate the petrified barrier, only the patient vigil of persevering attention— reverent, gently waiting. And suddenly the great stone would roll away and a newly risen human being would reach out to touch life again.

We need not be professional therapists, but we are all called to be a friend. All of us have that power. Whenever we pause—not to judge or advise, or even encourage— we need just to listen intently, perceptively. Hear this resurrection of a young woman who lost her way in the tomb of emotional pathology. It is a poem by Bonaventure Stefan entitled "Talitha Cumi," the Aramaic words Jesus spoke to the child he brought back to life: "Young woman, I say to you, Rise Up!"

I was not dead,
Not death marked by a stone

But I begged for the rest of burial.
Death—
I could not tempt his bony hand.
He looked for better company,
I volunteered for his corps,
Then groveled with guilt for asking.

Others were only human, as I—
Yet I was not,
Only the hull, the sham—
And this man could see it all.

I litanied to him my ills,
My oppressions.
They made me so—these people,
Twisting and contorting
Until my thoughts writhed
Like snakes in hibernation,
Or smaller than that,
Worms in a fishing can.

He listened—
No repulsion veiled his eyes,
No scolding, No hackneyed remedies.
Only the listening.
Intense, knowing, respectful,
With interjected "uh huhs"
That lullabied my fears.

His understanding
Became the hum of a dynamo—

The throb of another human's heart
Who did not shun me like a leper.
He listened and accepted,
Like the Christ of compassion
Who gave the people bread
When they had enough of words.

I could dare warm myself
At a flicker of hope.
His acceptance
Became an echo of "I thirst"
I saw my soul rise,
The void no longer yawned
With bottomless ugliness.
I felt the spark of life.

My life,
Accepted and meaningful
Another knew I lived
And now I knew it too.
I told the sun and the taxi driver
And shouted the news to the sky.
But the universe was too small for the joy
Exploding in my risen heart.

THOMAS OUR TWIN

Faith, like health, is most appreciated in its loss. Thomas must have been an unhappy camper—lonely, cranky, despondent, as he refused to believe in the new presence of Jesus. But he did not alter his mood to suit his company. He was not a people-pleaser.

Faith improves one's vision of life. It helps one see past the appearance of things and into their depth. Faith is what makes a marriage work when love has worn away—a belief in the other's integrity.

Religious faith can emerge in many assorted ways. For some it comes ready-made, like a prefabricated house. These are born into it, identify with it and have nary the need to question it. For others, arriving at a faith is a complicated journey involving assiduous study and tedious searching, full of detours and blind alleys. When this exploration ends in discovery, a whole new world opens. The celebrated English author, G. K. Chesterton (1874-1936), described his conversion as "turning upside down and coming upright!"

Something like this happened to Thomas, nicknamed Didymus, the twin. In the vernacular of academe, he had "cut class" and missed the fantastic resurrection appearance of Easter Sunday. A week later he was doing a "make-up," probably reluctantly, since he shared nothing of his companions' enthusiastic credulity.

Nonetheless, he showed up and so did the solution to his problem. Jesus happened to him. He was never the same since!

It is worth noting that this embryo church saw no reason to exclude the incredulous Apostle for his dissent; nor did Jesus. The episode points out that questions, doubts, even challenges about himself are welcome by Jesus. Notice how he responds to the person—not the problem—thus eliciting from Thomas the same oath that the Roman emperor, Domitian (51-96 C.E.) demanded of his subjects: "My Lord and My God."

Thomas undoubtedly felt disappointed in the Master. Cynical, let-down, indignant, he was probably driving on "empty" as he pushed himself to join his brothers. What if he had persisted in his dark temper and refused to be with those naive believers? He would not have heard the healing words of peace, forgiveness, and reconciliation. He could not have come alive again!

Thomas' disillusionment in Christ resembles people who have grown dissatisfied with the church. Once a solace, especially when those you needed to care didn't seem to, now the church holds little more than pledge drives, dull sermons, errant clergy and embezzling bishops. What's the use? There is nothing in it anymore. Quit going!

What to do? How about doing what Thomas did—"go on empty"? Something might happen! What's to lose?

Folks go to church for the wrong reason, namely, to be inspired. A better reason is to be inspirers. In the story *The Color Purple*, Shug asks Celie: "Celie, tell the truth: have you ever found God in church? I never did, I just found a bunch of folks hoping for him to show up. Any God I ever felt in church I brought with me. And I think other folks did too. They come to share God, not find him."

A faith is not something, it is Someone. Devotion to a creed is no substitute for intimacy with God. Dogma is not as important as is pragma—the sedulous practice of caring for human beings. A religion that is a quest for certitude is not a search for truth. There is no commandment, "Thou shalt be right."

Jesus gave himself personally and lovingly to doubting Thomas. This same solidarity with humanity continues today in the darnedest places, among the darnedest people, not just to the religious elite who regularly attend church. Check these words from a particularly surprising source. The turbulent, hard-living Irish actor, Richard Harris, wrote this moving appeal of Christ to the world in the early '70s:

I am not in Heaven
I am here . . . Hear Me
I am in you . . . Feel Me
I am of you . . . Be Me
I am with you . . . See Me
I am for you . . . Need Me
I am ALL mankind. . . .
Only through kindness will you reach me.

BODY LANGUAGE

The disciples were spooked at first sight of their fallen, now risen, Master. Phantoms frighten, so Jesus came to them as a guest, not a ghost. He dropped in for lunch. Now they could celebrate!

Among the wonders that Easter celebrates is the conspicuous reality of the human body. Western religions have not always been kind to it. The saints of old regarded flesh with grave suspicion—a treacherous tyrant ever demanding forbidden comforts. The appealing Francis of Assisi probably hastened his untimely demise by his pitiless corporal austerities. For centuries the Church encouraged harsh penance as a way of subduing the libido and thus placating its Author. Strictness was the antidote to laxness, but cold showers can stimulate as well as suppress.

Of course there is always the tendency in the human animal to overindulge and to waste inordinate time in the grooming process. Though vanity may be the motive, putting one's best face forward can also be considered an act of charity to the public. Beauty in any form always deserves a second look. So, what can be behind the current costuming craze to resemble a bedraggled refugee from the Klondike? Why are patched jeans more expensive than unpatched? Why are overalls de rigueur at the junior prom, or tennis shoes with a tuxedo? Such style statements are a bold declaration of independence away from the older generation, but they are not a blow for freedom from peer pressure.

It is not easy to look nice, especially if one's looks win no contests. One's fragile body can be an annoying nuisance . . . what with its imperious urges, its noisome secretions, its embarrassing excretions. And it falls apart so soon. That is why our bodies deserve the same patient compassion that Mother Teresa brought to the suffering poor of Calcutta. If incarnation means divinity took on a human body, it was surely not just from the neck up!

Why has mortal flesh received such indifferent press over the centuries? Six hundred years before Christ, the Persian Zoroaster proposed the theory that two external principles ruled the universe: light and darkness. This later developed into the Manichean heresy, namely, the dualism of matter (evil) vs. spirit (good). In this everlasting battleground, mankind is stranded in no man's land. Four centuries B.C., Plato resented the human body as a prison of the soul. Jesus taught that the body was innocent and that the mind concocted all manner of evil. Nazism was not invented by a body, but by a distorted intelligence.

The Easter mystery emphasizes the transcending importance of the human body. For Thomas Aquinas, the ultimate fate of the mortal person was the combination of body and soul for all eternity. This means that the Resurrection of Jesus is likewise the destiny of human beings.

To mistrust bodily instincts is sometimes the product of even sane religious training. Sensuality justifiably requires a caution signal. But there is a difference between sensuous and sensual. Jesus was sensuous; his senses worked for him. He felt grief and he wept; he felt terror and he sweat. He enjoyed children, a good meal and wine, laughter with his friends. He could be angry enough to throw the furniture around in the Temple. He was not ashamed of his emotions, including the negative ones.

Sensual is more a mental hang-up. Its focus is gratification and reduces the world to a playpen of infantile pleasure seeking. Play becomes more important than people. It is the offspring of fear and hysteria. Such jaded playboys and playgirls are too uptight to sip the wine of life. They gulp it down and are capable of only extreme, extravagant sensations that inevitably issue in ennui.

The body's five senses are meant to be experienced. They are singular instruments to bring us in touch with the stupefying grandeur of God's world. Physicality nurtures spirituality and vice versa. There is a whisper of wildness in all holiness. John Donne, the sixteenth century English metaphysical poet, caught the passion in the disciplined wholesomeness of the human heart bursting with longing for its Maker:

> Take me to You, imprison me—
> For I, except You, enthrall me,
> Never shall be free, nor ever chaste,
> Except You ravish me.

Be good to your body—trust its five senses. These know what your soul needs even better than your brain does.

SITCOM MOM

Happily or not, the modern media seems to have outgrown the *Ozzie & Harriet* depiction of family harmony. Situational comedy series about dysfunctional families spark the higher ratings. The trauma begotten of maternal extremes between pandering and punishing a child is unblushingly dramatized in the 1982 film, *Mommie Dearest.* The movie star depicted in the picture, Joan Crawford, would hardly win the "Donna Reed" award. A mother can be no more than she is as a woman, though her children expect perfection. Parenting appears to bring out the best and the worst in one's nature. Is there a more demanding vocation or broader education?

Mothers take the heat for parental failure more so than do fathers. But what man would apply for this job description?

WANTED: housekeeper—140 hour week, no retirement benefits, no sick leave, no private room, no Sundays off. Must be good with kids, animals and hamburger. Must share bath.

The irreplaceable Erma Bombeck added her typically matter-of-fact reality. . . . "No man could stand being pregnant. The first time a man lost his breakfast three solid months in a row, he would make plans to have a nocturnal headache for the rest of his married life."

Back in 1958, an indicting writer, Philip Wylie, rocked the public with a bestseller, *Generation of Vipers*, in which he charged that "Momism"—mother worship—was menacing the American Way. He emphasized that children should be raised to leave the nest. "To bring up children who are not dependent on you, it is necessary to indicate, from the start, that you, when you wish, can act entirely independent of them." This can mean that the couple is married to each other—not to the children. As someone sagely observed, "Good parenting is the product of good husbanding and wifing." Marriage and family is nature's seductive invitation to outgrow inherent narcissism. Females seem to have a head start in this process. Little girls are made aware of their future maternity in their early doll playing, but what boy is brought up to think of himself as a father-to-be? Wylie adds, "Fatherhood is the greatest male skill. But it cannot be picked up idly: it is not inborn." Neither is the talent for successful mothering. There is no crash course, no Motherhood 101. There is just the learning by the doing, which includes all the mistakes. Lucky is the mother who has married a father, not just a breadwinner. Some mothers do not have that support and have to go it alone.

Besides troubled marriages, mothers today must stretch themselves between kitchen and career. Fifty percent of modern moms will return to work outside the home before their child's first birthday.

Fittingly, a grateful nation celebrates Mother's Day. Fittingly also, today the liturgy features the Good Shepherd, which our mothers have been in most of our lives. But no place is more uncomfortable than a pedestal. Mothers would probably prefer understanding to applause. It took me 65 years to understand mine. . . . Tiny, weighing in at 110 pounds, she was nonetheless fearless, forceful, fiercely independent, explosive and quick with the hated strap. I could not forgive her for the humiliating sting of it. In her mid-eighties and widowed fifteen years, I knew I would have to look after her. Retired from federal service, I headed for my duty with the enthusiasm of a gas chamber victim. I decided to level with her—to put my lifetime of gripes and disappointments on the table. With the persistence of a prosecuting attorney, I enumerated my list in the face of her denials, defenses and tears. Then, she finally said something that turned me around completely. . . . "Do you want me to confess to you?" she firmly declared. "Well, you can whistle for it. I did the best I knew how to do, and that's the end of it."

Suddenly, I saw my self-centered self-absorption. I had only thought about me and I was sick of it. I felt a new inquisitiveness about my mother: how she saw life, what mattered to her, what her feelings were. I explored her recollections of grinding poverty in her native Hungary, escape to America at age fifteen, learning the language, factory labor, an unfulfilling marriage, the hand-to-mouth depression years, the determination to survive. We became friends. We finally enjoyed each other's presence. She died at 92 and the last five years of her life are a cherished memory for me.

From all this I learned two important facts:

1. You cannot love anyone you cannot be angry at.
2. You are only angry at those you care about.

A mother of thirteen was chided for claiming to love all her children alike. "We all have favorites. Which of the thirteen did you love the most?" she was asked. Her answer: "The one who is sick until he gets well. The one who is away, until he gets home."

We bless you, Mothers, for having so blessed us!

THE VINE THAT BINDS

"Never pass up a kiss," wrote Stan Burroway in a newspaper report some years ago.

In Pittsfield, PA, Roderick Long began to walk across a 50 foot long bridge over Little Broken Straw Creek on his way to work. His wife, Geri, had driven him to the span, but the bridge had been damaged by ice floes earlier in the day and he didn't want to drive across. Suddenly, Long turned around and walked back to his truck—he had forgotten to kiss Geri good-bye. Just then, the 25-foot center section of the bridge collapsed—the very part he would have been on, he said later, if he hadn't remembered the kiss.

This closeness of the Longs saved Rod's life. In the Gospel image of "Vine and Branches," Jesus is highlighting how intimacy with him can safeguard our spiritual lives.

Vineyard tending is a fine art. The University of California at Davis offers doctorates in viticulture—the study of vines, and in endology—the making of wine. Productive vines demand delicate attention. They need a special soil, a special climate and drastic trimming. Young vines are not allowed to produce for three years in order to increase the eventual yield. The implication is that a caring Providence allows life's rigors to prune us humans if we are to achieve adult specifications.

The vitality of the vine comes from its suitable grounding. Nurturance from the soil passes to the branches, which in turn energize the roots by absorbing sunlight and CO_2. The vine and the branches depend on each other. They are one piece. In fact, vine and branch appear indistinguishable. Separated, they perish. In this process, nothing is wasted. Even sour grapes are useful. Withered branches are good for kindling.

This lovely pastoral vinery parallel emphasizes the Creator's unity with Creation. Divinity is embedded in humanity. To see God, one needs only to look around. . . . Having attended church with his grandfather, the youngster asked, "Grandpa, can you see God?" "Billy," replied the old gentleman, "it's getting so lately, I can't see anything else . . ." Looking for God is like looking for the air, when all the time we are breathing it.

This means that no one is ever alone in this universe. Mankind is a mutually interdependent network. All living beings survive by complicity with other living beings. The great eighteenth century poet/preacher, John Donne, illustrated this intertwining hominal fabric when he wrote:

> No human being is an island entire of itself; every person is a piece of the continent, a part of the main. If a clod be washed away by the sea, Europe is the less. . . . Anyone's death diminishes me, because I am involved in humankind. And, therefore, never send to know for whom the bell tolls. It tolls for thee.

In John Steinbeck's classic, *The Grapes of Wrath*, a down-home preacher, Casey, utters these profound words:

> Tain't sayin' I'm like Jesus. But I got tired like Him, an' I got mixed up like Him, an' I went into the wilderness like Him, without no campin' stuff. Nighttime I'd lay on my back an' look up at the stars; mornin' I'd sit an' watch the sun come up;

midday I'd look out from a hill at the rollin' dry country; evenin' I'd pray like I always done. On'y I couldn't figure what I was prayin' to or for. There was the hills, an' there was me, an' we wasn't separate no more. We was one thing. An' that one thing was holy. . . .

God is holy because God is whole. We are only on our way!

FOUR LETTER WORD

Swahili has a dozen words for banana. There are separate names for ripe banana, picked banana, cooked banana, and so on. Why so? Because bananas are important to that culture. For the most important reality on our spinning planet, the English language has but a single overused word: love. People declare "love" for their cat, their canary, and their Camaro; as well as for God, baseball, and lemon pie. Enough, already! How about a moratorium on that indiscriminate term of endearment? Can we explore more exact expressions for our varied affections, perhaps caring, concern, cherish, regard, fond?

John's Gospel is awash with the word love. In today's brief reading, he uses it nine times. How should it be understood? The Greeks had a word for it—*agape*—the unselfish wanting good for another. No easy chore for the self-absorbed. That is why love is a commandment. Were it not an order from on high, our concerns would tend to end with the self. Jesus enjoined it because life demands it. There is simply no human development without love. Deprived of this essential nutrient, an emotional cripple is formed. . . . But can love be commanded? How can loving be a duty?

Nazi holocaust survivor, psychiatrist Victor Frankl wrote:

> In the living laboratories of the concentration camps, we watched comrades behaving like swine, while others behaved like saints. Man has both these potentialities within himself. Which one he actual-

izes depends on *decisions*, not *conditions*. Our generation has come to know man as he really is: the being who invented the gas chambers of Auschwitz, and also the being who entered those gas chambers upright—The Lord's Prayer or the Shema Yisrael on his lips.

To love, therefore, is an act of the will. To fall in love is common enough: to stand in love takes soul—resolution—a response to injunction.

A religion that teaches the positive acceptance of the self that I am, not the self I would like to be, provides the firm basis for loving mankind. The thirteenth century German mystic, Meister Eckhart, summarized this topic:

> If you love yourself, you love everybody else as you do yourself. As long as you love another person less than you love yourself, you will not really succeed in loving yourself, but if you love all alike, including yourself, you will love them as one person and that person is both God and man.

This is our high calling—why we were born—the shining privilege to be a friend to every human being. This vocation is sure to bring us life's inevitable twin offspring, joy as well as sorrow. But it will bring us to wholeness—another word for holiness. In the words of Kahlil Gibran: "For even as love crowns you so shall he crucify you. Even as he is for your growth, so is he for your pruning. When you love, say not 'God is in my heart', but rather, 'I am in the heart of God.'"

Maybe we overcomplicate this mystery of love. Even a child can understand it. A child is freely impertinent enough to make affection pertinent. . . . Early one morning a little girl tiptoed into her sleeping parent's bedroom and softly touched her lips to her mother's cheek. The abruptly roused mom gruffly chided, "How many times have we told you not to bother us at this ungodly hour?" The child: "I didn't come to bother you—I came to give you a kiss."

BREAKING UP IS HARD TO DO

A hand for Neil Sedaka!

When Romeo finally bid goodnight to his new flame, he could characterize parting as "such sweet sorrow" because he had just made another date with Juliet for the morrow. He would see her again. It was not so sweet for Bogart and Bergman to say good-bye in the classic movie *Casablanca*. Their farewell was final after a very ardent "hello." For those close to each other, it is a wrenching ordeal when the bond is abruptly sundered. When the person who opened your life to you is no longer there, you are once again half-alive.

When Jesus suggested that "those who mourn" are blessed, he could be saying how fortunate are those who have loved enough to grieve for a departed. The measure of one's grief is the measure of one's love.

In the movie, Bogie and Ingrid could opt for their poignant parting, because they were involved in a cause larger than their mutual affection—defeat of the Nazis.

The Ascension story is something like this. The disciples of Jesus had grown accustomed to his space among them. They never knew anyone like him: straight talking, perceptive, profound, unpretentious, astute, transuding God's Spirit. He was their guru. Dependent on his leadership, now he needed theirs. If they were to get his job done, it was necessary for him to go away. It was time for them to take on the world, but on their own.

Jesus' leave-taking was much like Inauguration Day as the outgoing transmits authority to the incoming president . . . or the colorful military change of command ceremony when the former CO hands the flag to the new commander. Jesus knew they would be distressed, but he knew the crisis was not terminal and that it could toughen undeveloped muscle. So he did not "poor baby" his unfledged emissaries, he exacted their marching orders.

Human nature readily tends to distrust autonomy in favor of authority, that is, the surrender of personal independence to a charismatic leader. Such abdication provides a temporary illusion of security. Jesus apparently did not wish his protégés to be easily-led sheep. He, therefore, encouraged questions, dissent, even challenges. He prized frankness. He rebuked Simon Peter for not understanding God's ways, but he never threw him away. Jesus knew it takes time to mature. He gave it all the time the process needed.

The Ascension message attests that the beautiful things of life are built into the ugly. Joy and sorrow are never far apart. In fact, one nourishes the other. It takes an ominous illness to elicit the sweet thrill of recovery. Chaos occasions order. Remedies are the offspring of disease. Glorious flowers bloom from the commonest dirt.

Maybe God's best-disguised gift to us mortals is life's custom-built crosses that never seem at first to match our dimensions. Suffering eventually tenderizes us. Another's heartache is more sensitively commiserated because of our own. Were it not for loss, what would we know of the loneliness that tells us who we really are when there is no one to hold our hand? When we come face to face with emptiness—when there is no place we feel we belong—it is then that faith bids us reach out to touch another lonely exile.

From his *Responding in Gratitude*, Rev. John D. Gondol describes a little boy plying his granddad with questions:

"Gramps, what happens when you die?"

Gramps explained it as best he could. Still puzzled, the boy asked, "Does that mean you won't be here anymore?"

Grandpa nodded, "Yes, that's true."

"Does that mean you won't be able to play catch with me anymore?"

"Yes, it does."

"Does that mean you won't be able to fly a kite with me anymore?"

"Yes, son, it does."

"Does that mean you won't be able to take me fishing anymore?"

"Yes, it does."

"Well, Gramps, when that time comes, who is going to do those things with me, if you're not here?"

The wise grandfather explained, "When that time comes, it will be time for you to do those things for another little boy."

BOMBSHELL PHENOMENON

Today is a day for balloons, streamers, and party hats. It's the Church's birthday. Celebrate!

Scripture attempts to describe the spectacular event metaphorically by employing the language of elemental forces: wind and fire. It is the evangelist's way of relating what happened when the Spirit of God zapped a handful of scared people, snapping them out of their frightened funk, inspiring them to turn their world upside down. This festival remembers the hurricane and flame that symbolizes God's Spirit connecting with man's.

Pentecost affirms that God is not a testy sovereign, impossible to please and poised to punish whenever human nature steps out of line. It attests that God is a thunderbolt of animation—boisterous, noisy, a high voltage happening, not an abstraction. God is a verb, not a noun.

The Pentecost God is playful, does not mind being misunderstood, and is not miffed when not taken solemnly. It is hard to imagine this God enjoying being treated as an oriental potentate—worshipped behind silken veils and smoky incense. Pentecost invites the world to lighten up about God, who is for us, not our adversary. That is why Jesus names the Holy Spirit Paraclete and Comforter—our defense attorney and support. Pentecost celebrates a good-humored Creator, perfectly willing to share the secret of sacredness with creatures.

The innovative first Pentecost announced to the wide world that the Spirit of God is not the exclusive preserve of any particular religion. An implication can be drawn that divinity welcomes fresh, unconventional ideas about Itself. Thus, it is not solely dependent on traditional, organized ritual to make Itself known. "The Spirit lists where it will" (John 3: 8). Religious orthodoxy need be no mental strait-jacket. Vitality, originality, naturalness appear to be as prized by the Deity as by ourselves. Whatever their status, Pentecost is a testimony that all human beings participate equally in divine dignity. Which means that groveling in guilt is hardly a tribute to God. Self-debasement can scarcely be praise to the One who cannot make junk.

Why is it so hard for people to appreciate their special-ness? Probably, because from birth, some of us have been brainwashed into believing that to feel important is a sin. Humiliation is seen as training for the real world. I, for one, was not taught to trust my judgment, but to prefer that of my "betters." This is standard strategy for a dominating authority that wills to maintain control. Thinking out loud for oneself is taken as resistance.

So, Pentecost emphasizes human preciousness and the latitude it thrives on. It invites the serious, searching mind to break new ground in religious thinking. It suggests that ancient formulations are not cast in cement—that new prob-lems require new solutions. It highlights that God does not condemn us for being human, any more than a parent would banish a child for spilling his milk. If we are born into imperfection, perfection can hardly be expected. Again, we are saved, not because we are good, but because God is.

To believe in the frolicsome, zestful god of Pentecost, one, therefore, need not turn a back on life in order to approach the holy. Living everyday—in the kitchen, the supermarket, the freeway, the office—is where God is encountered. Someone captured this blessed ordinariness in a prayer/poem discovered in the Chester Cathedral almost five centuries ago:

Give me a good digestion, Lord,
And also something to digest.
Give me a healthy body, Lord,
With sense to keep it at its best.
Give me a healthy mind, good Lord,
To keep the good and pure in sight,
Which seeing sin is not appalled
But finds a way to set it right.

Give me a mind that is not bored,
That does not whimper, whine or sigh.
Don't let me worry over-much
About this fussy thing called I.
Give me a sense of humor, Lord;
Give me the grace to see a joke,
To get some happiness from life
And pass it on to other folk.
Amen.

MEGA-GOD

A fourth grader questioned her rabbi: "Jews say the Lord is one. Catholics say God is three. Can you tell me when He'll be four?" The late controversial Episcopalian bishop of San Francisco, James Pike, once quipped: "Mohammedans have one God and three wives. Christians have one wife and three Gods." So much for informal levity about the Trinity!

Today the liturgy celebrates not a hallowed event, like Pentecost, but a "doctrinal" feast—Trinity. It refers to the fact that this dogma was developed centuries after the last word of the New Testament was written. The Hebrew scriptures have no hint of a triune God. What did the Church Fathers have in mind when they formulated a tenet important enough to begin and end every formal prayer?

As Christology developed in the first century Church, so did belief that Jesus was divine. Assigning divinity to significant personages has not been uncommon in human history. The Roman Caesars were claimants to this august attribute, as were Japanese emperors, until the end of WWII. The oneness that John's Gospel (10: 30) claims for Jesus with the Father, fostered this faith of his co-equality with the Godhead. Bitter were the disputes over this theology and much violent blood spilt, but defining the "Blessed Trinity" insured deity status for the carpenter of Nazareth. The feast of the Trinity did not become generalized until the fourteenth century. It is still unknown in the Eastern rites.

The early conciliar Fathers may have aspired to interpret for the world a God actively involved with it. The

Trinity was their answer. "Father" identifying providence, "Son," brotherhood, and "Holy Spirit," the medium joining the divine and the human. It was an elaborate attempt to have God appear more accessible, more personal. In fact, the "person" aspect was so emphasized as to include "three."

Alas, words are feeble. In the rare air of the mind, words are all that thoughts have to start them on their way. Theologians do the best they can with what they have to work with—frail language. Thus, abstruse formulations can result about the divine nature that often obscure more than they clarify. Jesus could best explain who his Father is by what his Father does. He used everyday figures with which his hearers were familiar. How to convey that God is to be sought less in ceremonial ritual than in the humdrum routine of daily life: in the kitchen, the bedroom, the freeway, the mall, the office? Trinitarian theology is a college try to this end, but a clearer message comes through since today is also Father's Day. Now hear this! . . .

Hello there, this is your Father, God, speaking. . . . Do you really want to know what I am about? You can study theology and the scriptures if you like, but I will let you in on a sure-fire secret. Try being a parent. There is nothing that will bring you in closer touch with Me.

I have shared My power to create with you, fathers. Like you, I was not certain what I let myself in for, when I created your kind: free to rebel or obey, to reject or embrace. It was a path you had never been down before, when you first became a dad.

Creating meant limiting My omnipotence, just as generating restricted your liberty. We both did it willingly. We both took a chance, and I'm glad I did.

CORPORATE TAKEOVER

Christendom is doubtlessly grateful that ceremonial religion has outgrown sprinkling people with bulls' blood, as recorded in this day's Exodus reading (24: 8). Jesus instituted a tidier ritual of God bonding when he initiated the Eucharist. Corpus Christi celebrates this event. What was in his mind when he declared the bread he blessed to be his body, the wine he offered to be his blood?

There can be no doubt that Jesus wanted his presence to remain in the world that he was leaving. He had been the Good News; it was now his disciples' turn. He clearly wanted them to be his extended living substitutes. In the 2 March 2000 edition of the Jesuit weekly *America*, F. Gerald Martin wrote: "Jesus did not institute the Eucharist to change bread and wine into his body and blood, but to change us into his body. The Mass is not meant to transform elements, but to transform people." In that same issue, a laywoman, Amy L. Florian, states: "Those who reverence Christ's presence in the Host must also reverence Christ's presence in human bodies." Implicit in Vatican II's Constitution on the Sacred Liturgy is the teaching that the words of consecration are spoken over the elements of bread and wine, as well as over the assembly. Thus, the presence of Christ becomes real through three forms: scripture, the Sacrament, and the believing congregation.

The emphasis is obviously to keep Jesus alive in our everyday lives, so he identified himself with the commonest staples of his day—bread and wine. Which can come down to this: what nourishes and refreshes us is Jesus happening to us. Eucharist, then, is not something we do; it is something we are. We can make Eucharist whatever has meaning in our lives—our loves, our labors, our losses, our longings.

No words are more important than those we say in our good-byes. At the final meal with his beloved Twelve, Jesus might have intended this farewell . . . "When you wine and dine together, when you are sharing and listening and laughing with each other, when you are having a good time, I am there." In fact, the original celebration of the Eucharist in the first century was more like a tailgate party. *Agape* it was called—"love feast." As numbers increased, so did problems. Snobbery in the ranks led to elitism. Some got high on the wine. To insure becoming behavior, the Church formalized the rite with a protective thicket of rules and prohibitions. Initially, lay people were chosen to preside over the Eucharist, including women. Subsequently, ordained clergy claimed that privilege exclusively. In later centuries, detailed auricular confession began to give a courtroom cast to the penitential rite. As the accuser and the accused, only the priest's absolution rendered the penitent "worthy" to commune, though reminded by the Liturgy just prior to receiving, "O Lord, I am not worthy."

This bread for the world was becoming more and more distanced from it. Enclosed in the tabernacle, or enthroned in a golden monstrance, the Sacrament became an object to be gazed at from afar but not consumed. It appeared that Jesus was being quarantined from contamination with the sinners he redeemed, as though getting too close to them would somehow corrupt God's morals. The faithful attend Mass these days not to kowtow to a conceited deity, or to be ranted at for being human, or harangued for money. They come for solidarity with a God that invented the Eucharist in a supreme attempt to humanize human beings.

A devout daily communicant was invited by her pastor to serve as a special Eucharistic minister. She was uneasy about this; would she do it right, maybe spill the Sacred Species? She acceded, however, and was a nervous wreck for her first performance. Gradually, the prayerful devotion of those to whom she extended the cup dissolved her tension. She was deeply moved. Later that week she was asked to help at a community soup kitchen. As she ladled the potage for the elderly needy, she felt the same reverence she experienced that Sunday offering the chalice. From then on, the kitchen stove became an altar for her.

Those blessed with a faith that sees in the Eucharist the Lord's desire for a friendly incorporation with himself, will understand the sentiment in this poem entitled "A Memory and a Hope":

> Often, tis true on my day's horizon
> I see in the east the clouds arise,
> But within my heart I carry a whisper
> That brings light o'er the darkest skies—
> A memory bright as a golden sunset,
> A hope as sweet as the fields in May,
> I am going to Holy Communion tomorrow—
> I went to Holy Communion today.
>
> Many a time I am weary of labor,
> Vexed with a life of work and worry.
> Tired of giving myself to others,
> Worn with the fret of this age of hurry—
> Then o'er my heart's unquiet waters
> Comes my Lord's sweet whisper to say,
> "We shall meet at communion tomorrow—
> We have met at communion today."
>
> Sometimes others are rough and thoughtless—
> Sometimes it may be hard and cold.

105

I long to pour out on the first quick impulse
All the pain that my heart docs hold —
Then my HOPE & MY MEMORY blended
Plead in my soul with a note of sorrow,
"Jesus lay on your tongue this morning,
Keep your story for Him tomorrow."

All day long like a ballad burden
Sings in my heart that musical chime—
All my minutes swing backward and forward,
Between that bliss of two points of time—
And I know the grateful heart on the Altar
Is touched to think my own is gay—
Just because He is coming tomorrow—
Just because He has come today.

LADIES' DAY

A harried young mother was beside herself when the telephone rang, but she listened with relief to the kindly voice on the line. "Hi, Sweetheart, how are you?"

"Oh, mother," the poor thing said, breaking into tears. "It's been an awful day. The baby won't eat and the washing machine broke down. I tripped down the stairs and I think I sprained my ankle. I haven't had a chance to go shopping and the house is a mess and we have company coming for dinner tonight."

"There, there, darling everything will be all right," the soothing voice on the line said. "Now sit down, relax and close your eyes. I'll be over in a half hour. I'll pick up a few things on the way over and I'll cook dinner for you. I'll take care of the house and feed the baby. I'll call a repairman I know who'll be at your house to fix the washer this afternoon. Now stop crying. I'll take care of everything. In fact, I'll even call George at the office and tell him he ought to come home early."

"George?" the distraught woman said. "Who's George?"

"Why, George! Your husband!"

"But my husband's name is Frank."

There is a pause; then the woman on the line asks: "Is this 555-1783?"

The tearful reply! "No, this is 555-1788."

"Oh my, I'm terribly sorry. I must have dialed the wrong number," the voice on the phone apologizes.

Another short pause before the would-be daughter asks: "Does this mean you're not coming over?" (*Connections,* June 1994)

Jesus agrees to "come over" to Jairus' house to attend his mortally ill daughter of twelve. On the way, he encounters a desperate woman suffering from a female disorder known as menorrhagia, a profuse menstrual flow, for as many years as Jairus' child has had life. This was an especially mortifying morbidity since in the Jewish culture it rendered the victim "ritually unclean." She was forbidden worship in The Temple. Whoever she touched incurred official pollution. She had to keep her distance. "If I but touch his clothes, I shall be cured." In the jostling crowd she reached for her relief. . . . The Torah recommends no less than eleven prescriptions for healing this ailment. Among them was a superstitious nostrum of carrying a burnt ostrich egg in a linen rag. . . . Her contact was instantly efficacious and Jesus was aware "that power had gone out of him."

Helping hurting people is not without cost. To reduce another's pain, one must be willing to allow it to pain oneself. Compassion means suffering with the sufferer. . . . Jesus did another subtle favor for the recovered woman. He invited her to confront her embarrassment. She did so and enjoyed a richer liberation. A culture that prizes concealment and camouflage over upfront disclosure is a society of disguise and subterfuge. To confront is to care enough not to overlook a problem, but to look it over candidly together. It is the opposite of condemnation.

It is not hard to identify Jesus as a feminist. He had no trouble dealing with women as equals in that repressive patriarchal age. Centuries later the battle of the sexes wages on. Men who are uncomfortable with feminine equality simply are afraid to learn about themselves. Team-personship sounds more useful than a competitive stalemate. Samuel Johnson (1709-84) admitted: "Nature has given women so much power that the law has very wisely given them little." In the words of Charles Dickens: "If the law supposes that," said Mr. Bumble, "the law is a ass, a idiot." It is a strain, however, to understand how female fulfillment is enhanced by doing more and more of what men do. Women surely deserve their executive chairs, or even, at last, president of the U.S.A., but firewomen, combat Marines, prize fighters? . . .

Appropriately dubbed the "Womens' Gospel," the next scene is the home of Jairus. On the threshold of womanhood, his daughter is now dead, and the professional mourners are in full swing, rending pre-torn clothes and wailing to the tune of flutes, would you believe! They jeered Jesus for not joining in, but put-down or applause never seemed to turn his head. He took charge of defining himself and did not abdicate that responsibility to others. This self-assurance is noted in his recommendation to Jairus: "Do not be afraid, just have faith."

Faith in what?

It was probably reckless of this respected synagogue official to openly affirm the suspect Nazarene. I hear Jesus urging the grieving father: "Take a chance on what you believe in—however politically incorrect—a miracle can happen!" And it did.

A miracle of our time is the about-face of the infamous apartheid in South Africa. For nearly thirty years, octogenarian Nelson Mandela was a political convict. He is now Prime Minister of the nation that imprisoned him. Check the Christ-like confidence in his inaugural:

Our deepest fear is not that we are inadequate. Our deepest fear is that we are powerful beyond measure. It is our light, not our darkness, that frightens us. We ask ourselves, who am I to be brilliant, gorgeous, talented, fabulous? Actually, who are we not to be? You are a child of God. Your playing small does not serve the world. There is nothing enlightened about shrinking so that other people won't feel insecure around you. We are born to make manifest the glory of God within us. It is not just in some of us, it is in everyone. And as we let our light shine, we unconsciously give others permission to do the same. As we are liberated from our fear, our presence automatically liberates others.

WISDOM OF WEAKNESS

A hit on the road, Jesus was a flop in his hometown. His neighbors were admittedly impressed by his words, but not with him. How important can a blue-collar person be, or one of questionable parentage, to a snooty audience? "Is he not the carpenter, the son of Mary? To mention only the mother's name, for the Jewish mind, was to imply illegitimacy. Even the Gospel records the conception of Jesus to be out of wedlock. Joseph also had a problem with this.

Novelists find small town narrow-mindedness a favorite theme. Sophisticated urbanites are no less hobbled by this cramping mentality. To restrict one's view of an individual only to the limits of social classification, is to miss the unique surprises in every personality. The town folk dismissed the impact of their native son because they stereotyped him. They labeled him out of a significance which is the malevolent basis for all the horrors of racial injustice: holocausts, lynchings, apartheid, ethnic cleansings!

To the religious right, who regard as sacrosanct archaic traditions of another age, disregarding up-to-date prescriptions for current problems, stereotyping is an occupational hazard. Jesus reducing the 613 precepts of the venerated Mosaic code to a simple three-pronged commandment: love of God, self, and others. This might have been a bit too left wing for the neighborhood. "And they took offense at him."

How did Jesus handle this rejection? According to *The Way* edition of the Bible: "And he could hardly accept the fact that they wouldn't believe in him." He is obviously hurt, but does not sulk. He moves on to a more receptive audience. In fact, he empowers his disciples to go out two by two to see if they can do a better job than himself. And darn if they don't (next Sunday's Gospel)!

Stereotyping is a form of prejudice which decides not to examine the unfamiliar. It is the obstinate conclusion to remain inflexibly down-on what one is not up-on. Pious believers who crave certainty will never search for truth. They settle for a God of no surprises who behaves like they want God to behave: rewarding the "good guys" and punishing the "bad guys." The "hanging judge" type! A faith that needs to know what will happen next is hardly faith. Mature faith does not need to know. It does not cling. It lets go. It takes a chance without a net. It leaps!

Which brings us to another intriguing bungee-jump—Paul's free-fall into the mystic insight of the wisdom of weakness. Again, *The Way* edition: "For when I am weak, then I am strong—the less I have—the more I depend on him." The Apostle is saying that all our mortal flaws, failures and frailty are in God's plan for us. We creatures are the Creator's opportunity to be creative. When God made human beings he created co-creators. Creation is still going on. Check the recent DNA discoveries! God continually shares His creativity with us a little at a time, just as parents share their knowledge, experience, and values little by little with their children as they grow.

No caring parents throw their child away for spilling his milk, hitting his sister, or breaking a window. The lapse provides the parent with the chance to show how to hold the glass, how one is liable to get hurt when hurting others, or that the window will be repaired from the youngster's allowance. Responsibility is the message, not reprisal. When the teenager can't stand the sight of the parent because he or she is reminded of being a little kid, the adult knows this will pass. The adolescent has to revolt to discover how revolting the process is.

Paul is saying God is no less savvy. He is affirming that human imperfections do not alienate God from His creatures anymore than a child's inadequacies separate them from a good parent. It simply elicits greater attention. The good God knows that mortal existence is a delicate balancing act between our assets and liabilities. Lighten up, he urges in his first Corinthian letter (1: 27-29):

> Instead God has deliberately chosen to use ideas the world considers foolish and of little worth in order to shame those people considered by the world as wise and great. He has chosen a plan despised by the world, counted as nothing at all, to use it to bring down to nothing those the world considers great, so that no one anywhere can ever brag in the presence of God. (*The Way*)

MISSION IMPLAUSIBLE?

The lifestyle that Jesus imposes on his on-the-job trainees would never rate the "Savvy Traveler's" seal of approval. No baggage, no carry-on, no second shirt, and no extra underwear is certainly the weightless way to go, if hygiene is not a high priority. He did not want them to stall for arguments on the way, or to waste time looking for the "light on" at Motel 6. Keep moving, he insisted, and count on the hospitality of the town folk—a social duty taken very seriously in Eastern culture.

It was not that freeloading had any special appeal, but it presented an opportunity to be on a level with the people— to be with them, not above them; even to be subordinate, needy. Let them care for you, Jesus intended. The exchange is to be bilateral: bread and board for heart and healing. Listen to their perceived demons: anger, abuse, fear, the taxes, the children, the in-laws, the boss! Healing can more readily happen around the kitchen table than from pulpit to pew. Get close to people, be a presence of peace—you need no more than your heart and your head!

I came closest to this communal ministry in the active service. The chaplain lives with the men: sharing their dangers, their discomforts, their longings for safety and for home. He was not always welcome at first, but if he brought the presence of God to their foxholes, and to their ship's battle stations, they did not want him to leave. It reminded me of the description of a missionary given by Bishop James Walsh, a Maryknoll founder: "To be a missionary is to go where you are not wanted, but needed and to stay until you are wanted and not needed."

Traveling light takes getting used to. Did you ever have to move out of a commodious dwelling into a tiny studio apartment in a strange city, because the job you needed transferred you? Remember the tearful packing of your precious possessions for storage? A year or so later when a promotion offered you a less cramped existence, you sent for your storage stuff. As you began opening the sea of cartons, you may have wondered, "What in the world was I thinking when I packed all this? I haven't needed any of it . . . the clutter is back." Sometimes life deprives us of what we think we want, so that we can discover whether we really needed it.

Possessions have a way of possessing their possessors. But life's most leaden load is reserved for the stockpile of bitterness. According to William Sloane Coffin (*The Heart is a Little to the Left, p. 5*), "In fact, it's comforting to be bitter. But it's not creative, bitterness being such a diminishing emotion. . . . And some people can't live without enemies: they need them to tell them who they are." There are those who collect injuries like trophies; medals of honor for "mayhem endured." The habitué in line at life's complaint counter might more usefully examine an unconscious need for punishment. The self-imposed verdict of guilt for a past secret shame can keep one's antenna on constant alert for offense, whether real or imagined. The tragedy of an abused childhood can have the same crippling effect.

Jesus advises his messengers not to harbor hurt. "Whatever place does not welcome you or listen to you, leave there and shake the dust off your feet. . . ." He is coaching them not to allow the rejection of one town to contaminate their enthusiasm for the next enterprise. Junk all grudges—find a new start—past poison has no place in the present. Quit playing the victim and give resentments a respectful burial!

The traveling orders of Jesus are less a program of austerity than a blueprint for freedom. The unladen life takes little comfort in the abundance that spawns demons of worry for guarding and getting more. The contented career is convinced that wealth is not things, but people. Jesus did not command the world to be holy, but to love more. Traveling light is to live one's life lightly, lovingly: to connect to everything, to everyone, but to belong to oneself. There is another world but it is in this one.

To the so-called orthodox, whose tastes tend to the reassurances of institutional, formalized religion, Jesus' proposal for a mendicant ministry must sound highly implausible. But to those heralds who enjoy uncomplicated contact with the locals, it is simply the one Mission Possible.

TAKE FIVE

"Come apart and rest awhile" is the old translation of Jesus' invitation to revive weary disciples after their missionary debut. When burnout feels like "coming apart" at the seams, relaxation becomes an illusive luxury. In fact, despite the bounty of leisure endemic to the American way, we are far from a people of rest. Foreign cultures are agape at the frenetic pace of American tourists. They seem to pity what strikes them as an American dread of being still.

Perhaps Americans identify stillness with boredom, so empty spaces must be filled. Oscar Wilde said once: "To do nothing is the most difficult thing in the world." We were trained to value busyness: "idleness, the devils workshop"; "time is money"; "at least look busy." But "rest" is a surprisingly popular four-letter word in the Bible. Even God takes a day off (Gen. 2: 2). The popular 23rd Psalm is a veritable lullaby of sweet repose. Jesus promises rest to the work- and worry-weary of the world: "Come to me you who are heavy laden" (Mt. 11: 22).

Why do we fight being still? Could it be that is when our inner demons are most apt to get our attention? We all qualify for factory recall, but we can never fix what we don't know is broken. I am most restless when particularly dissatisfied with myself: for my impatience, insensitivity, self-centeredness. Formerly, the tendency was to look away, or to futilely resolve to change, or to blame others for the way I react, and disquiet increased. Since, I have learned to hold still: stop, look and listen to me.

A friend shared an acronym describing this holding pattern: HALT, it is called. H stands for hungry, A for anger, L for lonely, T for tired. Whenever these are experienced, stop whatever you are doing, make no decisions, stall and thoroughly feel the mood, however upsetting. Allowing it changes it. Do not argue with it or tell it what to do; let it tell you what needs doing.

When the self does not care to be heard, an emotional fog bank ensues that one can get lost in. Confusion only seems more comfortable than confrontation, but the denial defense is exhausting. Developing an ear that hears oneself is the first step on the journey to the center of oneself. St. Augustine (354-430) thought this trip worthwhile; "Recognize in yourself something within, within yourself. Leave aside the external life: descend into yourself. Go into that hidden apartment, your mind. If you are far from yourself, how can you draw near to God?" Myth maven Joseph Campbell saw centering the mark of a champion; "The athlete who is in championship form has a quiet place within himself, and it is out of that his action comes. If he is all in the action field he is not performing properly. There is a center out of which you act. . . . Unless the center is found, you are torn apart and tension comes." (Interview with Bill Moyers)

In his remarkable study of *The Varieties of Religious Experience*, Henry James (1811-1882) analyzes the profound spirituality of "letting go."

> Passivity, not activity; relaxation, not intentness, should now be the rule. Give up the feeling of responsibility, let go your hold, resign the care of your destiny to higher powers, be genuinely indifferent as to what becomes of it all, and you will find not only that you gain a perfect inward relief, but often also, in addition, the particular goods you

sincerely thought you were renouncing. . . .
Something must give way, a native hardness must
break down and liquefy. It is but giving your little
convulsive self a rest, and finding that a greater self
is there. (James pp. 98-99)

The healing process of centering oneself can be
achieved by way of the meditation process. Simply get
comfortable. Put your eyes at half-mast. Turn off any tape
playing in your head and focus on your breathing . . . in, out,
in, out! If a thought bubbles up to consciousness, make no
comment, no judgment, just allow it to drift away as you
make a meaningless sound to yourself called a "mantra,"
such as "Om." The habit of fifteen minutes of daily meditation can effect a gentle restoration that reduces heart rate,
metabolism and high blood pressure.

Sometimes we do not slow down until life knocks us
down. Should illness make you hostage, may this tranquil
advice, from Grace Noll Crowell's poem entitled "For One
Who is Tired," come through:

Dear child, God does not say today, "Be strong."
He knows your strength is spent. . . .
And so He says, "Be still, and know that I am God."
The hour is late, and you must rest awhile,
and you must wait
Until life's empty reservoirs fill up—as slow rain fills
an upturned cup
Hold up your cup, dear child, for God to fill.
He only asks today that you be still.

CATERED AFFAIR

It is hard to reconcile this Gospel with Jesus' repudiation of the temptation to bedazzle his public with miracles. Matthew and Luke clearly report this disavowal in their fourth chapters, wherein prior to his public career, Jesus wrestles with the decision to take his chances proclaiming the Good News without attendant bewitchment. He obviously wanted people to believe in his message, not his magic. He wanted to be seen as a teacher and a healer, not as a sorcerer or magician. How then are we to take this loaves and fish story? What are we to believe about it?

This stupendous multiplication account must indeed be important. It is the only miracle narrated in all four Gospels. Most scholars generally agree that it offers a conspicuous reference to the Eucharist. But first, the miracle issue . . .

The Bible is a tidal wave of miracles: the Red Sea parting, the Burning Bush, the Walls of Jericho, Jonah and the Whale. The New Testament perpetuates the plot: water to wine, the dead revived, fabulous feedings of multitudes. Ancient biblical authors wrote in an age of scientific unsophistication. They were not interested in proficiency concerning nature's laws. Their tendency was to surround significant events and personages with exceptional details to highlight their prominence. Fact and fiction were interwoven to the delight of the audience, largely illiterate. Authors used extravagant marvels as a literary device to explain mysterious phenomena—the transcendent, the indefinable! It was their way of dramatizing the awesome presence of the spirit of divinity. Similarly, the evangelists employ "miracles" to set Jesus apart as a divine presence and beyond the cosmic standards of the Creator. By arousing admiration to him, attention is drawn to His message.

Miracles did not seem particularly important to Jesus, judging from his advice to his disciples to soft-pedal any publicity about them. He knew that miracles did not change people that much. The 5,000 free-lunchers would be hungry the next day . . . the restored dead would have to die again . . . the celebrants at the Cana water/wine tasting could have awakened to a hangover. To focus on the miracles of Jesus is to separate him from human emulation. The same spirit that filled him was to fill his followers. His same compassionate concern for people that few wanted to deal with—cripples, bag ladies, streetwalkers, criminals—was to be the preoccupation of his church. Kindness is the miracle with which we can identify, not the prodigies of Superman!

As previously mentioned, the loaves and fish proliferation is a distinct referent to the Eucharist, the center and essence of Christian worship. Eucharist is from a Greek word meaning "thanksgiving." This suggests the appropriate attitude for receiving the Sacrament—gratitude! Thankfulness for having made it thus far in life; for a faith that helps make sense of it; for the chance to grow and learn to love.

What qualifies one to receive this sacred gift? Confession, absolution? However devoutly shriven, the Liturgy reminds the faithful just before communing: "O Lord I am not worthy." What prompted Jesus to feed the vast throng? They were hungry! And what human being is not hungry for meaning, for filling the vacancies in existence, for the Goodness we call God? Mary Carolyn Davis glimpses this wistful quest in these lines:

When the sun shines in the street
There are many feet
Seeking God, and all unaware
That their hastening is a prayer.
Perhaps these feet would
Deem it odd.
(Who think they are on business bent)
If someone went and told them,
"You are seeking God."

It is no surprise, then, that the Eucharist should come to the world in the form of food. What is more basic to life than eating? This fundamental habit rates exceptional space in the Bible. Even the hereafter is described as a "banquet." Eucharist, as bread, asserts that God wants to be our nurturance—to be ingested and assimilated into the most commonplace human activities: our working, our relating, our suffering, our dying, and our enjoyments, like the pleasures of eating.

The miraculous supply of provisions for 5,000 proceeded from a very modest source—a young lad's picnic lunch of five barley buns and two fish. Amazing what God can do with little when given with good heart! On December 1, 1955, Rosa Parks probably didn't think she was doing very much when she refused to give up her seat to a white man on that bus in Mobile, Alabama. Her decision to stay put, respect her conviction, and accept the consequences, sparked the racial justice revolution worldwide.

We may feel that we are not much, but the little each of us have is all God needs to make miracles happen.

PEAK EXPERIENCE

A little polar bear in the frigid Arctic questioned his mother, "Am I a real polar bear?"

"Of course you are, dear," she responded.

He then asked his father, "Am I a real polar bear?"

"Certainly you are!" his father answered.

Unconvinced, the little guy put the same query to his grandfather, grandmother, and cousin polar bears. The puzzled mother polar bear confronted her youngster, "Why are you incessantly questioning whether you are a real polar bear?"

"Because," he replied, "I'm freezing!"

This child's waggish bedtime story serves to introduce a notion relative to the gospel Transfiguration story—not everyone is comfortable in his native environment.

Jesus apparently adjusted to the Roman occupation, but there were some things he did not like about the religion in which he was raised. He obviously objected to a piety that placed ritual conformity above human necessity. Over the centuries, the 613 precepts of Moses hardened into a hidebound manifesto for every aspect of orthodox behavior that hobbled more than hallowed Hebrew life. The inflexible restrictions, for instance, of Sabbath observance were not taken seriously by Jesus, so he was seen as subverting the Law. By-the-book religions tend to degenerate into legalism. For Jesus, persons enjoyed priority over precepts. He refused idolatry to injunctions. Just as Thomas Erskine

127

of Linlathen once observed, "Those who make religion their God will not have God for their religion."

Jesus saw religion as a celebration of life, not an IRS audit. His spirituality embraced a God who was an enthusiastic companion to the human condition—a willing copartner in ongoing Creation. For him religion was not a moral code or a system of ethics, by which salvation was earned. Eternal life was a wedding party to which everybody was invited. Nor did he seem convinced that exemplary morality guaranteed divine approval. Prostitutes and criminals warmed to his message more so than the righteous right, who put out a contract on him.

Jesus brought a whole new lightsome touch to the old-time religion. That is one way to think of the Transfiguration on Mt. Tabor. It was a peak experience for his favored cabinet, Peter, James, and John. They understood him at last! They finally put it all together! How could the evangelist more dramatically describe their sudden, glorious insight, than in a blaze of incandescent splendor! The ancient law-giver, Moses, was there to affirm the new covenant with Jesus. The great prophet Elijah, who Jews believed would return to earth to introduce the expected messiah, was on hand. The entire scene receives a resounding "Amen" from the Divine cloud!

This apocalyptic scenario allegorically implies that any living religion is subject to the process of all living things: growth, development and therefore, change. To be animating and relevant a faith needs to be open to newness—to fresh ideas. Jesus emphasized commitment to the brotherhood of all mankind. The Old Law highlighted Jewish exclusiveness. Paul consistently repeated the Christ-vision to the reproach of die-hard traditionalists. "In this new life one's nationality or race or education or social position is unimportant: such things mean nothing" (Col. 3: 11).

The Vatican II Council had a similar breakthrough impact on Christendom. Many resent the changes, but the Church needed to reexamine its relevance to the modern world. As Mark Twain once remarked, "change is only comfortable to a wet baby." The religious right preferred a church they remembered: strict, sovereign, fixed—frozen! They saw the conciliar Church as "getting soft" when it was actually inviting the faithful to a deeper, more mature spirituality; easier access to the Sacrament, fraternal respect for other religions, fuller involvement of the laity. This church accepted that its theologians do not have the last word on the understanding of God or the mystery of life. It outgrew the fortress mentality and saw itself a wayfaring "pilgrim" in pursuit of truth, not its sole possessor.

In the hilarious one-nun production *Late Nite Catechism*, the audience laughs uproariously at the ritual practices of fifty years ago. Will fifty years from now find the piety of this generation just as funny? Why not! Certifiable pilgrims keep moving. If they are not open to learning, to newness, to growth, to change, they have but one option—rigor mortis!

RUNNING MATES

If you were in the audience when Jesus said, according to the evangelist, "I am the bread come down from heaven," what do you think might have been your reaction? I would most likely notify the analogous "911" of the time, to get a net! Can you blame the murmuring? . . . "Is not this Jesus, the son of Joseph? Do not we know his father and mother?"

Why did Jesus make this spectacular claim, knowing full well disbelief was guaranteed. His Twelve were just as dismayed, but they hung in with him. They knew there was more to him than just a local carpenter. They did not understand any more than the others but they trusted him . . . Maybe that is what faith is about! It is easy to believe what is usual and understandable. The "incredible" demands greater investment.

When Robert Frost penned the lyrical lines, "The woods are lovely, dark and deep, But I have promises to keep, and miles to go before I sleep," he touched on the plaintive, human pique about life's unfinished business. There is always more to be done when the journey finally ends. That is why Jesus commissioned disciples to perpetuate his message and instituted the Eucharist to preserve his presence. He saw his Good News as nourishment for the world. He obviously personally identified himself with his message and called it the "bread of heaven." He never hedged from this extraordinary deposition. In fact, he testified to it all the more in the face of the perturbing bafflement from followers. Jesus presented a simple choice: he was either nutrition for mankind or just a nut!

Even more astounding is the correlation to this credence: namely, that whoever acts with the heart of Christ is also "bread of heaven." Wherever there is compassion, consideration, and courtesy for another, his presence comes alive. Jesus insisted on solidarity with those who value what he valued.

> Anyone believing in me shall do the same miracles I have done and greater ones. . . . You abide in me and I in you. . . . Because I will reveal myself to those who love me and obey me. The Father will be in them, too. We will come to them and live with them (John 14: 12, 12, 20, 21).

This is not an appeal for saintliness, just common-place sensitive humanness. A few examples . . .

> An elderly passenger is holding a bouquet of fresh cut flowers. He notices across the aisle a sad-eyed young woman, obviously troubled and depressed. Each time she glanced at the flowers her expression brightened to a wan smile. As the old gentleman prepared to leave the bus, he dropped the cluster in the young person's lap. "I can see you love flowers," he said, "I think my wife would like you to have them. I'll tell her I gave them to you . . ."
>
> From the window the young lady saw the old man enter the gate of a cemetery by the side of the road. *Bread of heaven!* (Told by Bennett Cert)

The March 2000 issue of the magazine *Maturity* features an interview with the famous movie star, Martin Sheen, describing some of his charity activities. One of them is a full day service, once each week (when not on location) at a refuge for the homeless in Venice, CA. When elected honorary mayor of Malibu, he organized this elitist beach town to be a sanctuary for the homeless—to the consternation of many of the natives. I recall a memorable evening with the actor when we were both guests at the rectory of another social activist, Fr. Bill O'Donnell, Berkeley, CA. Martin explained: "Acting is what I do for a living—social justice work is what keeps me alive." *Bread of heaven!*

Even tiny tots can nurture. Brenda W. Quinn had this story in *Catholic Digest* a few years ago:

> It was one of the worst days of her life. Newly separated, she was tired, sick, lonely, hot (it was July) and discouraged. It was all she could do to lift her little boy into his highchair for dinner.
>
> She put his food on the tray and began to read the mail. Another bill she could not pay—it was the last straw. She leaned her head against the tray and began to cry.
>
> The little boy looked at his sobbing mother very intensely, then took the pacifier out of his mouth, and offered it to his distraught mother.
>
> She began to laugh through her tears and hugged the source of such total unconditional love. *Bread of heaven!*

Teachers can be bread of heaven. As Bradley Miller observed: "Teaching a child not to step on a caterpillar is as valuable to the child as it is to the caterpillar."

Eucharist creates equality with Jesus. It is his friendly, mutual corporate takeover. Recently both major presidential candidates made a considerable fuss about choosing running mates. The Lord is less discriminating—whoever wants to be, is his running mate!

RITE STUFF

The midsummer Eucharist refresher course grinds into the fourth week of John's sixth chapter. One more week to go! The recurring reprise: "I am the living bread come down from heaven: Whoever eats this bread will live forever: and the bread that I will give is my flesh for the life of the world." This thoroughly startling language obviously shocked the Jews who heard it, but the pagans familiar with the ancient mystery religions of the near east would barely blink an eye.

In his study of *The Gospel of John* (Volume 1, pp. 221-222), William Barclay describes pagan worship of animal sacrifice.

> Once the flesh has been offered to the god, it was held that he entered into it: and therefore when the worshipper ate it he was literally eating the god. As the people rose from such a feast they went out, as they believed, literally god filled. . . . The one thing the Mystery Religions offered was communion and even identity with some god. . . . In the Mysteries of Mithra the initiates prayed: "Abide with my soul: leave me not, that I may be initiated and that the holy spirit may dwell within me." In the Hermetic Mysteries the initiate said: "I know Thee, Hermes, and thou knowest me: I am thou and thou are I." In the Mysteries of Isis the worshipper said: "As truly as Osiris is not dead, his followers shall die no more."

Sound familiar?!

Mithra was the ancient Persian god of light; Hermes, the Greek messenger of the gods; Isis, the Egyptian goddess of fertility. Isis' brother/husband, Osiris, was believed to have come back from the dead. Even resurrection was not original with Christians! Pagan rituals were carefully staged to provide maximum emotional impact: music, incense, lighting. Participants were obliged to undergo lengthy instruction and intense ceremonial purification in preparation for these rites. This historic religious phenomena highlights humanity's everlasting longing for unity with divinity. Times have little changed!

Why this besetting preoccupation? Perhaps for the same reason a child likes to identify with Superman or Harry Potter . . . because the child feels small, impotent, unqualified for independence. Consequently the child assigns outsized superiority to the parent in order to feel safe. Should such emotional deficits perdure into adulthood, authoritarian religion presents a strong appeal. It provides a life plan, a moral code, a system of ethics whereby salvation may be earned. It attracts those who want to be led: left-brain type thinking that values structure, dogma, law and order. When directives become imperatives, legalism is bred and minimal compliance evolves, but for the free spirits resistance is activated, while the passive-aggressives content themselves with silent sabotage.

People who do not wish to wrestle with life's absurdities and incongruities will prefer security-blanket religion to launching-pad spirituality. Jesus obviously wanted a more mature faith from his followers. He did not value servile submission so as to gain authority approval. He taught illustrative stories that elicited right-brain speculation, creative conclusions, spontaneity, and openness to newness. He accentuated ideals over edicts, initiative over habit.

Maybe that is why Jesus made such staggering claims about his "flesh" and "blood" as universal nurturance? Maybe he wanted his hearers to get past his words and to him personally. The world is starving for the compassionate presence of Christ! How could he more specifically will that sacred human presence to the world than by integrating his body with our own?

We may never be invited to the White House for a state dinner, or to the Court of St. James for tea, or breakfast at Tiffany's, but John's sixth chapter offers one clear invitation: "Come to my table, I've been saving a place for you. Relax, loosen your tie. Tell me all about it. I am here for you—body and soul, flesh and blood—just yours. Let's put them together!"

STAFF AND STUFF OF LIFE

The exhaustive five week series of John's sixth chapter, in the heat of August dog days, has finally crescendoed. To share something fresh on the subject of Eucharist each Sunday, has been a daunting chore, but eminently worth the effort. Making God partisan and an accessible accomplice to the human enterprise is the reason why the Sacrament exists at the center of Christian worship. Eucharist is entente between God and mankind.

Why the relentless drumbeat of words that shock and disgust? Consuming human flesh and blood is clearly cannibalism—an unthinkable endorsement by Jesus. So, what did the Johanine authors have in mind when they assigned these astonishing statements to the Lord?

A possible elucidation could be the evangelist's effort to counter Christological heresies that were muddling the infant Church. . . . It is quite typical of neo-converts to overdo. Flushed with the fervor of renascence, they often tend to overcorrect for past errancy. Extreme cases make up for lost time by embracing an almost virulent probity. Puritans are commonly indicted for such militant zealotry. The Puritans of the early Church were a group known as "Docetists." They overspiritualized Christ by denying his humanity. For them his physical body was only an appearance—not real. Another elitist group in the growing Christian community were the Gnostics. They believed that only by special knowledge, imparted to the few, was salvation available. Both factions rejected the humanness of Jesus, thus equating him with an ethereal being that objected to being contaminated by any mortal involvement. The official Church refused to allow Jesus to become an abstract theological hypothesis. His life was not meant to be a mythic fiction, left on the shelf of history. He was a living book, to be thoroughly read, indeed, consumed! So the gospel emphasizes the flesh and blood of Jesus to accentuate his humanity and his total participation in the human experience.

Eucharist is an affirmation of the physical body—the soul's sometimes troublesome but inseparable companion. In the wholesome compound of mind and matter, the communion table does homage to the dinner table, even to the pool table and the card table. Material creation continues to be infused with divine approval. "Then God looked over all He had made; it was excellent in every way" (Gen. 1: 21).

Eucharist celebrates life and lifts vision beyond creaturely touch, taste, sound and sight. Each communion is a rite of passage from self-absorption to awareness of fellow beings—an invitation to adulthood. It highlights "the man for others" and a deity that welcomes coalescence with human nature.

The ritual of communing is no guarantee that the communicant will be magically transformed for the better; no more so than the nuptial ceremony guarantees a good marriage. Each day spouses need to renew their pledge to each other. To receive the Eucharist fittingly is to resolve to value what Jesus values—to love what he loves—people!

True love never runs smoothly. Misunderstandings are simply inevitable.

> Many of Jesus' disciples who were listening said, "This saying is hard; who can accept it? ... As a result of this, many of his disciples returned to their former way of life and no longer accompanied

him. Jesus then said to the Twelve, "Do you also want to leave?" Simon Peter answered him, "Master, to whom shall we go? You have the words of eternal life."

As in marriages that last, conflict is the precise time not to split. Disputes confronted and issues openly dealt with can mold a deeper, stronger bonding. The late Malcolm Muggeridge, brilliant editor of *Punch*, was raised an atheist. A sharp-tongued social commentator and television controversialist, this witty scoffer had little use for church or churchmen. Toward his life's close, he experienced an astounding change of heart. Skeptic Malcolm confessed to an invasion of his consciousness by the sheer beauty and sublimity of Christ's life as related in the Gospels. His 1975 book, *Jesus*, is an elegant expression of that improbable illumination. He wrote:

> Man's effort to make himself happy in earthly terms is doomed to failure. I have concluded after having failed in past experience, in present dilemmas, and future expectations. As far as I am concerned, it is Christ or nothing.

Simon Peter came to the same conclusion!

TYRANNY AND ORTHODOXY

This gospel recalls a *New Yorker* cartoon depicting a very nervous candidate for celestial citizenship. As the pearly-gatekeeper reviews the applicants' life record, St. Peter keeps exclaiming; "No, no that's not a sin either. My goodness, you must have worried yourself to death!"

Religions have a way of making sins of the most harmless human behavior, like ball games on Sunday or hamburgers on Friday. I ruefully recall the church of my childhood. Life was one hopeless rulebook. Whatever seemed to be fun was labeled a transgression. What was not a sin was forbidden. For me, the Almighty was a cosmic schoolyard monitor—forever poised to punish for laughing in church or whispering behind Sister's back.

Seminary training further validated this rationale. Pastoral care focused more on admonishing idealistic perfectionism than solicitude for flawed humanity. Even prayer was taught like a binomial theorem. A mathematical exactitude was preferred to spontaneous, lighthearted accessibility to God. Later, as a confessor, I was stunned by the quagmire of guilt in which so many penitents were mired for just being human.

A penitent myself, I confessed time after time, "unchaste thoughts."

"Are you avoiding the occasion of sin?" queried the confessor.

"No," I responded, "I have to hear confessions, and the only thing I hear are sins of the flesh—I get ideas!"

Experience took its time, but reality eventually set in. I can honestly affirm after fifty-five years of priesthood and thousands of confessions, I have yet to hear a mortal sin. The traditional conditions for committing such are "grievous matter, sufficient reflection, and full consent of the will." I could never certify the coalition of these three requirements as occurring simultaneously.

Clinical psychologist Father Marc Oraison, OP, criticizes the moral theology taught in that past era in his 1968 book *Morality For Our Time* (p. 44):

> ... (M)orality is defined without the least mention of God. (Mindful of Paul to the Galations and Romans). It is neither the law nor its observance which saves. On the contrary, the law although good in itself actually kills. It is grace, that is to say love, that is our salvation.

How then did the Church get so hung up on moralistic coercion over the centuries, when Christ's Good News is so plainly humane, balanced, and lighthearted? His parables gush with God's limitless mercy. Guilt and censure are barely in his Father's vocabulary. This gospel episode has something to say about regulatory gridlock . . . . It illustrates mankind's impulse to relieve painful insecurity by escape to the sanctuary of doctrinaire religion. Here, there is no dirth of official masterminds who mask their own flight from personal inadequacies with their drive to dominate the "sheep," and are perfectly assured of doing God's job for Him! Jesus openly revolts against this style of ecclesiastical despotism. He objected to religious leadership that convoluted rational regulations into meaningless taboos.

The Mosaic injunction for handwashing before eating is simply a healthy caution for nomadic wanderers not too preoccupied with hygiene, much the same as parents persistently hound their youngsters to pre-meal ablutions. But institutions change over time because their leadership does. Authority can complicate by overcorrecting. . . . Not only were hands to be ritually cleansed before eating, but between each course! During enemy sieges, when water was pitifully scarce, devout Jews preferred to die of thirst rather than drink what was needed for ceremonial purification.

Jesus objected to this orthodox tyranny. He trusted the intrinsic autonomy of a good heart more than extrinsic compliance to authority. And so he was a menace to dogmatic traditionalists of a bygone era. Discipleship for Jesus meant responsibility; the ability of conscientious response to human need. He favored deliverance from repressive judgment and morbid culpability. He most likely had no argument with regimentation as a good thing for organizations, but not for fellowship. His church fares better as a household than a powerhouse!

"NONE SO DEAF . . .

. . . as those that will not hear," said Matthew Henry (1662-1714). A century before, the adage aficionado John Heywood wrote:

> Who so deafe or so blinde as he
> That willfully will neither heare nor see.

Two psychiatrists meet for a drink after a long, hot day. One is utterly wilted and worn out—his hair tousled, his face drawn, his clothing rumpled. His colleague, however, is composed, nattily dressed and completely at ease.

"Rumplemeyer, for heaven's sake," the first psychiatrist says incredulously, "how do you do it? I'm completely done in and you look as fresh as a spring morning. How can you look so great and be so composed after listening all day to peoples' problems, fears, anger, unhappiness and neuroses?"

The second doctor smugly sips his highball and then responds, "So who listens?" (*Connections*)

This Gospel deals with deafness and its attendant speech impairment. They are usually concomitant. When sound is not heard neither is one's own voice, which then comes out indistinctly. Deafness is generally more embarrassing than blindness. People are inclined to be more considerate with the sightless than they are with the hard-of-hearing. Having to shout can be annoying. Jesus is sensitive to this condition and takes the deaf-mute aside to avoid any public mortification.

Listening is a very fine art. It takes practice. But it's the way to learn about oneself. Self-knowledge is rarely accurate, since one's opinion on oneself is rarely objective. Many of us would like to think of ourselves as we should like to be—not as we are. We are most often influenced by others' impression of ourselves, which, at best, can only be a partial assessment.

Still, most of us wish to be thought well of, so the tendency is to put our best foot forward and to conceal deficits. This leads to a defensive maneuver—induced deafness—whenever we do not want to hear a negative message. Nothing infuriated my mother more than the deaf ear my father exploited to her nagging.

Self-induced deafness is the protective ploy of the passive-aggressive personality; averse to making waves, too timid to confront, peace is settled for at any price. For such, getting involved spells hurt or at least defeat. Thus candid interrelating suffers, and the leading troubled marriage complaint ripens—poor communication. The exasperating indifference of detached types occasionally gives way to caustic sarcasm and ridicule, but the underlying hostility is seldom met head-on. Collisions are devoutly avoided, and pacifiers are pursued in excessive eating, drinking, sleeping, working, reading, overexplaining and cozy religion, to name a few. These illusory escapes succeed in keeping the desired distance from others, but more unfortunately, from oneself, and do little to improve an inner sense of worth.

The non-confronter sees nothing positive about anger. St. Augustine identified it with hope when he wrote that "hope has two beautiful daughters, anger and courage."

To refuse hearing is to refuse hope. To hear no evil is to close oneself from the real world that is in constant need of renewal.

I create my own deafness whenever:

1. I make fun of you so I do not have to take you seriously.
2. I make myself busy to avoid involvement.
3. I pay no attention to my own negative emotions—anger, anxiety, annoyance.
4. I overexplain an embarrassing moment or mistake when a simple "I goofed" would do.
5. My monologue competes with yours and I refuse to allow your opinion.
6. I'm afraid to try for fear of failing or crying for help.
7. I label you; discount you with a category that prejudice inspires.
8. I seek noise, distraction, or intoxication to drown out what I don't want to hear.
9. I pray for miracles before exploring my own solutions.
10. I forget God and I are partners.

We learn to love by listening—to ourselves as well as to others—however faint the whisper or frightening the thunder. All of us need hearing aids in this world's cacophony of sounds. One that works for me is the belief that when I harken to the one that wants to talk to me or shout at me, I am listening to God!

HOW TO WIN FOR LOSING

The setting for Simon Peter's inspired declaration of Jesus as messiah occurred in the heart of pagan territory. Northeast of Lake Galilee, Caesaria Philippi, once called Balinas, was the center of Baal worship. Up on the hillside was a cave believed to have been the birthplace of Pan, the Greek god of nature. Further up the slope gleamed the white marble temple dedicated to the ruler of the world, the Emperor Caesar, now regarded as god.

At this time the Jews dreamed of a messiah, an anointed, menacing, militant monarch who would reduce the enemy to its knees in homage to conquering Israel. Longing for a liberating messiah is everyone's dream, especially for the oppressed. And deliverers do appear—a Lincoln, a Gandhi, a Martin Luther King. Awesomely, they seem to share a common lot—liquidation. When Jesus knew this would happen to him and talked about it, Peter was upset to think that the repugnant enemy could overcome an invincible messiah.

Life is just not fair! There are consequences to human behavior, but sometimes evil deeds escape retribution and good deeds are capriciously penalized. The sacred writers attempt to make sense of the puzzle of why the innocent suffer by introducing the involvement of God. Still, the mystery persists. While it is impossible for me to applaud a parent who wishes pain for a child, it is just as unthinkable to worship a God who wills the cross for His "only begotten son." I can, however, honor a parent whose heart breaks as he chooses to allow an errant offspring to do jail time for speeding tickets ignored, or for selling drugs, or for repeatedly driving under the influence. Youngsters need to learn. "Tough love" may be as instructive a mode as any. Does a loving Father witness His creatures suffering knowing that tragedy is never the bottom line? We count on a God that will somehow extract victory from the jaws of defeat.

Calvary unravels the mystery: good is made out of evil. God's bewildering providence is a clear sample of "tough love."

Jesus knew that the mind of God values the valor of the "suffering servant" over the heroics of the victorious warrior. He believed that when the chips were down, the dark forces of entrenched power would not be allowed to prevail finally over its victims. Does God then will suffering? Does the caring parent? Both recognize that ordeals can be redemptive, in fact, ennobling, so they do not protect their charges from whatever can lead to the triumph of the human spirit. That is why Jesus could say that losing one's life in a good cause is a way of finding one's true self. Sydney Carton, of Dickens' *A Tale of Two Cities,* comes to mind. He substitutes himself for the guillotine so a condemned friend can escape to marry the woman they both love. Graham Greene's moving *Power and the Glory* tells the story of a failed "whiskey priest" who finally finds reconciliation when he knowingly risks a trap to arrest and execute him as he ministers to a dying man during the brutal Mexican persecution of the 1920s.

But these are tales of fiction. The martyrdom of Central America's Archbishop Romero is grim fact. So is the murder of Father John A. Kaiser, a 67-year-old Mill Hill missionary, who was an outspoken advocate of human rights in Kenya, where he worked for 36 years.

Since martyrdom is neither hoped for nor foreseen in the sunset of my days, I shall attempt penetration to my best self by abandoning the impulse for self-importance. I should like to accept who I am—as I am—and let go the self I wish I was.

The world-renowned cellist, Yo Yo Ma, demonstrates understanding of this insight. Among his many glorious concert achievements, he is proudest of his appearance on Sesame Street, where he taught Elmo how to play the violin. The wife of one of his friends, Gert, lay dying of cancer. With his cello, Yo Yo visited her in the hospital and played one of her favorite Bach fugues. For her husband he brought a flask of fine scotch. Gert had a notorious penchant for pickles. Again Yo Yo visited her with his cello, but this time she was in and out of consciousness. The husband announced to his drowsy wife, "Yo Yo is here with his cello. What would you like, Yo Yo or pickles?" "Pickles," she responded sleepily.

Yo Yo left his cello and returned a half hour later with six jars of assorted pickles. The vanity of genius was swallowed by sensitivity to suffering. Yo Yo was never more of a virtuoso!

TEACHER CHILDREN

The tenderness of Jesus to children actually flew in the face of the common values of the time. In the Roman-Greco civilization of that day, children had zero status. They were the sole property of parents who could dispose of them as they pleased. To exterminate them or to sell them into slavery was not illegal, in fact, the word used in the New Testament for child is the Greek word *paedion*, also the word for "servant." Most servants were slaves in that era. Since children enjoyed even less rights than women, Jesus, in his gospel, assigned them for top priority care and attention.

The disciples argued about who was the most important among them. Jesus selected the most vulnerable "nonperson" in their presence to highlight the precedence that powerlessness rated with God. Numero uno or last place appear to rank on a par in divine appraisal.

As a compulsory celibate, I watched my sisters' families grow, and often felt deprived of the education raising children could afford. Having retired from federal service in 1980, my chance to be a deputy dad presented itself. Friends were going on a three-week cruise and offered their house for me to babysit, along with their two children. This episode is reported in the "Father's Day" chapter of the A cycle in this series. Suffice it to say, I flunked my paternity audition. Kind neighbors that I had appealed to for advice in my parenting dilemmas smilingly comforted me: "Don't feel too badly, Father, no one can take over in the middle of another's chess game!"

But I learned a few things. Typical of first-time parents who are anxious to do it right, I focused more on me than understanding the children. I wanted another chance.

At a recent overnight hospital stay, sleepless, I chatted with the night nurse. Interested in my points of view she finally asked, "What is the one thing you most want to do in your life?" I think she was expecting me to say, "Be pope, or bishop, or the chaplain on *Love Boat*." She seemed surprised, but pleased, when I answered: "I should like to care for a child."

I learned the following from my abridged surrogate parent venture:

1. The one thing that frightens children most are adults.
2. The saddest tragedy for a child is to be belittled. If a host would not think of humiliating a guest in their home, why a child?
3. The parent that does not allow a child privacy dooms the child to it forever.
4. The parent needs to be a good teacher. Teachers teach subjects; good teachers teach students.
5. The young need firm authority. As in handball, there's no game with a spongy wall.
6. Parents cannot expect children to appreciate the sacrifices they make for their young. Children never asked for them.
7. Real education is finding out for oneself. Children learn least when taught most.
8. The parent acts most like a child when the child is expected to be an adult.
9. It is not useful to teach children to be phonies, demanding they kiss someone not trusted, or to make a fuss about a gift not liked.

10. Never shush a child's questions. The universe fascinates them.

Children are quite at home with the idea of God. A mother asked, "Why is God hidden?" Her ten-year-old responded, "Because He wants you to look for Him." An eleven-year-old wrote:

> Dear God, I think You should listen to confessions in person. That way bad people would not try to get away with murder.
> Hi,
> George.

I have to agree with G. K. Chesterton in his uncommonly fresh *What's Wrong With The World*, written at the turn of the past century. According to G. K., what's right with it is that women are superior to men, not because they outlive us, but because they are closer to children, therefore, to life and nurturance. He decries the feminist ambition for equality with males. He deems this a step down for females. He also laments women who deplore the restrictions of domesticity, for to him there is no more important spot on the planet than a home. No government can be more supreme than a household and no wealth richer than a child. Each one born is God's testimony that He is not finished with us yet!

CLIQUE CLUB

This is one industrial strength gospel! In the first part, Jesus claims no exclusivity in demon expulsion for himself or his affiliates. The second part is stark Mark, headlining millstone drowning, terrifying endless torture and ghastly self-mutilation. Mark has Jesus speaking a language of jolting hyperbole, thus accentuating the enormity of malevolence. The words are not to be interpreted literally.

Drowning by millstone was especially offensive to Jews since it was a form of Roman execution. . . . Gehenna was the garbage dump outside of Jerusalem. It was situated in the valley of Hinnom, just south of the city, where the hideous sacrifice of infants to the god Moloch had been practiced. Gehenna was the Jewish figure for the nether world of retribution for evil behavior. The smoldering trash heap was used as a metaphor characterizing the consequence of a corrupt and wasted existence, much as when we describe a misspent life as "going down the tubes." Such a reprisal is no more the direct punishment of an offended deity than is a hangover from overdrinking. Nature has its own inflexible justice system.

The repugnant recommendations to self-mutilate in order to obviate evildoing persist in saturating the reading with extreme overstatement. This excessive language is intended to emphasize the resolute decisiveness vital for avoiding evildoing . . . the Galilean healer of the blind, crippled and lame could hardly advocate seriously such self-violence.

Back to the "members only" part of the gospel! The Christian churches of history have not been notorious for their sufferance of each other. For more than four centuries the Roman Catholic Church has been a "closed shop"—a tight union refusing to recognize the validity of any other faith. Sixty years ago seminarians tastelessly nicknamed their washrooms "Martin Luthers." Thanks to the Vatican II Council of the early sixties, this contemptuous intolerance died the death it deserved, and amicable ecumenism flowered forth. In 1986, Catholic churches joined their Lutheran brothers and sisters in celebrating the 450th anniversary of the birth of Martin Luther. In 1999, Pope John Paul II published his encyclical *Ut Unum Sint* ("that they may be one"), soliciting input as to how the papacy might proceed for the new millennium in the interest of Christian unity.

The Sunday *Los Angeles Times*, 28 Nov. 1999, printed a book review on a biography of the current pontiff by its religion writer, Larry B. Stammer.

> In John Paul's Christian humanism, human dignity is inherent because we (and all creation) are created by a living and sovereign God, the First Cause. Even non-Christian religions, the pope wrote (stirring up much consternation within the Vatican), are reflections of one truth. Though the paths may be different, John Paul believes that, to the extent that they tend toward God, they reflect the deepest aspiration of the human spirit to find its fullest dignity in God.

It comes as a surprise, therefore, that the Vatican should issue a recent 36-page document, *Domine Jesus*, accentuating the superiority of the Catholic Church over other denominations. Because it is the "mother" of all Christian churches, the Church of Rome claims the fullness of

Christ's Spirit, consequently preeminence, and the monopoly on salvation.

The issue is not whether the claim is valid, but how important is it in this day and age of growing mutual deference and interaction among the churches? Vincibility would seem more conducive to empathic dialogue than infallibility. Bridges are not built by one with all the answers and needing no discussion.

Why is it so hard for the human animal to tolerate the outsider? Is the turf worth the flak? Does not every independent soul march to its own drummer? Was it Martin Sheen who said: "Choose your enemy carefully; who he is you will become." Jesus, the ecumenist, along with Moses, had no trouble sharing religious authority: "For whoever is not against us is for us."

The English statesman John Morley (1839-1923) put it well:

> Toleration means reverence for all the possibilities of truth. It means acknowledgment that she dwells in diverse mansions and wears vesture of many colors and speaks in strange tongues. It means frank respect for freedom—the indwelling of conscience against mechanical forms, official conventions, social force. It means that charity is greater than faith and hope." . . . Religion need not be afraid of liberty and its lovely sister *tolerance*! The word "catholic" still stands for the opposite of narrowness.

HEARTS THAT PART

The Lord God said: "It is not good for the man to be alone."

Did this first line in this day's first reading ever spark an argument among the legendary desert hermits of old? They were solitaries, but they did not feel alone. They lived with God. It is interesting to note that in the Genesis Creation story, before Eve, in Eden Adam walked alone with God, and God concluded that even God was not enough for Adam. Neither were pets. Human beings need human beings, if they are to learn to be human.

So the story goes, God made a woman from the rib of Adam. To court a tired pun, she is not a side issue. She is every bit the equal of her man; bone of his bones, flesh of his flesh. Another interesting point is the usage of the word "rib." In Arabic, *rib* is the word for "close friend." Unfortunately, history has not always supported the biblical contention of male and female equality. Women enjoyed virtually no legal status in Jewish culture. They could be divorced for the flimsiest whims, which could account for the strict constraints Jesus urged in the matter of divorce.

Things are quite different for women in this day and age. Today they can make their own living and survive quite comfortably without dependence on the male of the species. It was not so in Jesus' time. Without family they were without protection. Jesus' stern stand on divorce was likely an attempt to safeguard feminine social stability. With the eventual cultural shift toward independence, and less need for a protective policy for women, what might be his attitude about unhappy marriages today? In his day marriage partners were commonly selected by parents. That system seemed to work as well as today's free choice. In fact, statistics indicate that the option to freely choose marital mates presents a higher risk for failure. Three out of five marriages are currently legally dissolved. For Catholics the number is one in five.

Affection dies, communication dead-ends, and relating dries up—how would Jesus handle these things? When all reconciliation efforts are beyond repair, surely Jesus could understand the heartache of a marriage turned sour. The reversal of an adult life's major investment is no minor tragedy. Human beings have a built-in longing for a fulfilling life-love—one that lasts. So why is this appetizing aspiration so rarely appeased? It certainly takes a grownup to see him or herself in the daily full-length mirror that conjugal relating involves. Once the "I do's" are ventured, there is no place to hide!

A California rabbi, who is a skilled counselor, has rescued many a foundering relationship. For the irreconcilable he has devised a "ceremony of parting" in order to obviate cold legal dissolution and bitter courtroom wrangling. In the presence of some close friends or family, the couple stands before him. He reminds them to cherish the good moments of their union and to forgive the hurts. He charges them to part as friends and to pledge themselves to caring parenting (if they have children), and never to speak ill of each other. They return tokens of their marriage, such as rings. He invokes a blessing for the past and for their future, and they part.

The Church could well use this pastoral concern for the separated. Divorced couples need help in dealing with their children. Studies show that the effects of a divorce influence the offspring more in adulthood than as a child. They have trouble trusting lasting relationships. Emotional stability comes more slowly, though they tend to be more successful in professional careers.

Divorced couples need help in the matter of candor with their children. Adolescents especially want to know the issues that were tried and why they failed in their parent's marriage. Youngsters often resent being treated as calendars, having little to say about scheduled weekends with the absentee parent. Advice about a collaborative divorce employing a single lawyer for both parties is also useful financial information.

Some think that the Church's annulment procedure is a canonical cop-out for divorce. Actually the word "annulment" is a more accurate term for marital dissolution. In the Church's thinking the validity of the Sacrament depends on conditions of freedom from force and the adult ability to make a permanent commitment. When either condition is lacking, there simply never has been a sacramental marriage.

The only relic of Eden older than sin is marriage. It is the school for maturing; the best chance to outgrow human nature's inbred narcissism. The one element that makes a human being human is personal relating. Intimacy needs more than a physical body; it needs heart and head and soul! The world is swamped with disposable products—disposable diapers, dishes, even underwear—everything but disposable people. As a plant that has withered through neglect can never be brought back to life, so marriages can run out of gas. Though many may opt for divorce, there is one thing for sure Jesus will not allow—divorce from himself!

SAD ABOUT BAD? GOOD!

Back in the '30s a *New York Times* featured an obituary. A deceased wealthy Park Avenue dowager had rated several columns, along with the widespread curiosity: "What did she leave?" Everything!

On a back page a lone, scant paragraph reported the passing of a very popular Little Sister of the Poor. What did she leave? Nothing! She took everything with her—her scrubbing the hovels of the needy, cooking their meals, attending their children, nursing the dying. She took it all with her.

This Gospel, about the rich young man, revived this story. He had everything going for him: wealth, success, and virtue. He even had the spontaneous affection of Jesus, who offered him something he did not offer many—a personal stake in the share of spreading the Good News. But his possessions possessed him and he passed up the invitation of a lifetime.

Imagination tends to range about this fellow; he appears to be a portrait of a nice guy. Proverbially they rarely finish among the winners. He must have been sincere, however, if Jesus liked him. But what moves one to ask the question he asked? Was he bored, disenchanted? Was "Is That All There Is" his theme song? He seemed successful until that fated query: how do you get to heaven?

If one has to ask that question, one better be prepared for some unwelcome advice. There is never a dirth of gurus who are sure they have the right answer. When one does not trust one's own judgment about a life path, one can easily be duped by a charmed shaman ever ready to lead the way. As the suicides of Jamestown, Waco, Texas, and La Jolla, California tragically attest . . . The enormous success of stellar star Elvis Presley was marred by a baneful life flaw. A biographer alleges him as a "momma's boy," which led Elvis to a passive dependence on parent figures. Maturity trumps worldly success every time!

What makes life rich? Probably not possessions. Rabbi Harold Kushner wrote in his book *When All You Ever Wanted Isn't Enough*:

> Our souls are not hungry for fame, comfort, wealth or power. Those rewards create almost as many problems as they solve. Our souls are hungry for meaning, for the sense that we have figured out how to live so that our lives matter, so that the world will be at least a little bit different for our having passed through it.
>
> If a person lives and dies and no one notices if the world continues as it was, was that person ever really alive?
>
> I am convinced that it is not the fear of death, of our lives ending, that haunts our sleep so much as the fear that as far as the world is concerned, we might as well never have lived.

Robert Louis Stevenson had this to say about living:

> That person is a success who has lived well, laughed often and loved much; who has gained the respect of intelligent people, and the love of children; who has filled a unique niche and accomplished his or her task; who leaves the world better than before, whether by a perfect poem or a rescued soul; who never lacked appreciation of the

earth's beauty or failed to express it; who looked for the best in others and gave the best he or she had.

Simplistic, perhaps, these quotes, but as artless as wisdom!

The most promising element in this rich person episode is his dejection: "And he went away sad, for he had many possessions." The depression he experienced for declining Jesus' offer could be the beginning of his maturity. As unwelcome as depression is, it deserves attention. It has much to say about what is missing in life. When not a pathology needing clinical treatment, sadness needs going into, not around. It is as natural to avoid feeling sad as it is to detour a bad conscience. If one is sad because of a bad conscience, it is not because one is bad, but because one is good . . . The malicious lose no sleep over their evil. Only good people have bad consciences!

POWER: A MEANS, NOT AN END

"The meek shall inherit the earth, because they won't have the nerve to refuse it" quips the wag, and adds that pushy people will get the parking places. Such is life in the big city! James and John, cousins of Jesus, were more this pushy type. They were not nicknamed Sons of Thunder because they were wimpy lightweights. They were nervy enough to lobby for the premier parking spaces, next to the Lord himself. "We want to sit on the thrones next to yours in your kingdom," they said, "one on your right and the other on your left."

As with most aggressive asserters, this brazen cheek does not sit well with the other brethren. Mark has Jesus using this situation to teach a lesson in bonafide *chutzpah* (Yiddish for "boldness"). "As you know, the kings and the great men of the earth Lord it over the people, but among you it is different. Whoever wants to be great among you must be your servant." This is not to advocate shrinking or cringing, but taking charge at being useful. To be in command is to guide, not subdue; to direct, not dictate. Authority, for Jesus, is the ability to serve.

This Gospel implies that the luxury of winning the top spot is only for openers. This status involves willingness to dare, to depart convention, to reexamine tradition, to suspect applause. It means consulting constituents, but not being controlled by them. It suggests constant evaluation of what is lawful for what is good; of what worked in the past but doesn't work now. Character trumps charisma. (Hitler had the latter.) Superiority ministers to inferiority.

There is no drug more intoxicating than power. We are well advised to beware of those who have to have it. To those so addicted, challenges to city hall are regarded as civil rebellion. Nor do they trust a competency that can supplant themselves.

Leadership is a function and a relationship. The function deals with the situation; the relationship, with people. People tend to follow the leader they know knows them as well as the situation. There needs to be a bonding between the leader and the led. They do not necessarily have to have a beer together, but subordinates need to know that they are cared about. In the military, officers are rigidly segregated from the enlisted, but a good officer is prized by the men. Marine Corps officers, for instance, receive the same rigorous training as do recruits. The officers do not eat until the men are fed. When a trooper requests an audience with the chaplain, his officer is on the phone: "This is no invasion of confidentiality, padre, but is there anything I can do?" The men know they are cared about and will not be abandoned. Wounded are never left alone. Even the dead were carried on the long, frigid trek from the Chosin Reservoir to Hungnam, Korea in 1950.

The Gospel is saying that for special privilege there's a price tag. . . . Want the height, can you handle the heat? Can you look at the worst and get to work? The future is no more secure for the top dog than for the underdog. The sweet smell of success evanesces about the same for both.

Some young people find churchgoing a bore, but are genuinely spiritually oriented to offer themselves for solid humane intervention. A group of teenagers conceived an extraordinary ministry. They agreed to look after muscular dystrophy victims so that their fatigued parents could get a break and the handicapped teenagers could have a chance to be with their own peer group. Wheelchairs were loaded into vans and off they went for rock concerts or camp-outs.

If Jesus is believed to be the true image of God in human form, then his values are God's. In his own words: "I am here not to be served, but to serve." Could God be interested in doing less? It is, therefore, hard to understand how God rejoices in being worshipped as Almighty and Omnipotent, unless God's power means limitless love. Therefore, believers glory in the Power not as an end to be worshipped, but as a means—having the capacity to love totally, unconditionally.

TWENTY-TWENTY

Blindness is oppressive, but then, so can be sight. The assertive Jericho blind man probably found that out for himself when cured of his sightlessness. Pleading for sight from the passing Jesus, he got what he wanted. In fact, it is the last miracle recorded before the death of Jesus. Bartimeus now had eyes to see this hideous spectacle. What would his life be now that he had to earn a living? Begging took no talent. Apparently he had spirit, since he was not embarrassed to make a noisy ado for what he set his heart on. Jesus habitually rewards persistence. "What can I do for you?" he asks the blind man. He addresses the person, not the ailment, and asks nothing from him.

Bartimeus refused to cop out to the crowd demanding him to hush up. Like an ignored hurt child, he cried all the louder. It paid off. . . . For those who equate insistence with arrogance, the tendency is to discount their own needs and consequently live under their potential. They are inclined to relegate themselves to the unthreatened bench and never get in the game. To want not, is to be not disappointed. This wary logic arrests the daring challenge to go for it, and passion idles in neutral.

Seeing is a sensory stimulus that elicits varied reactions. Some sights induce automatic denial. Jacqueline Kennedy's spontaneous words at the first sight of her mortally wounded president/husband: "Oh, no!" Some sights paralyze action, others activate instantaneous animation. It quite depends upon the nature of the beholder. As the sage observed, "we do not see things as they are, but as we are."

Vision, therefore, is a highly selective process. We see only in fragments. Terrorists see mainly their cause, not the agony they cause. Blamers can notice your faults, but not their own. Violators grow apathetic to their violence. Cultured SS officers, at the Nuremberg trials, testified how they got used to the atrocities they inflicted. Our own gun-goofy nation has its own perception distortions. The killer Bowies and Billys of frontier fame are not only celebrated in folklore, but even in musical comedies. Sports fans pay top dollar to witness violent mayhem in the boxing ring, the gridiron, the roller rink, and at the speedways. One of the worst terrorists in American history, who killed 168 people in Oklahoma City, was a decorated serviceman. Masses of Native Americans and African Americans have tasted extra-judicial retributive American violence—lynchings. Current gay bashing, thrill crimes, and child and spousal abuse enflesh the mystery of evil that has perpetually cursed the human race.

The big picture is generally the work of a committee of eyes, each contributing that separate detail that captures an individual's attention. Awareness of the universe is a global enterprise. Scientists, poets, and aborigines each have something to say about it. Living and surviving is a corporate venture and blind spots are a collaborative concern. To look is not always to see. Blind spots obscure vision.

Blind spots are ineffectual, often unconscious, defense maneuvers. Take overreacting, for instance, which involves an exaggerated response to a perceived threat. The tension could be sex, or alcohol, or authority, or mother-in-laws, but this enemy must be attacked and vanquished if the overre-actor is to feel safe! Such a person is blind to the unconfronted fear within. The scapegoater is blind to the unrecognized "chicken" within. "Mr. Milk-toast" on the job, "Attila the Hun" at home; hostility is vented on the intimidated. The rationalizer does not see the deceit in spurious excuses. "I don't go to church because of all the hypocrites there."

Seeing is not all that comfortable. There are those who watch, with aching hearts, the disfigurement and deterioration of a slowly dying loved one. The ordeal of daily attentiveness exceeds the courage of battlefield bravery. Their conscientious caring plumbs new depths in their humanity, conferring a sensitive conviction of the inestimable pricelessness of human life. . . . This is to stand in the Holy of Holies!

Faith is a visual aid. Faith wants to see what God sees, to believe what God believes. Seeing is believing. Like Bartimeus, when the blind spots dissolve, we are surprised at what we really look like. Faith says, "Getting to know you is getting to like you." As God does. It's even a bigger surprise to discover how worth knowing each one of us really are!

THE GREATEST OF THESE

Can love be commanded? Can one be ordered to love a cad, or even not to behave like one? Do commandments work? . . . Only when they are affirmed! The doctor's order for bed rest is especially efficacious with an exhausted patient.

But is it possible to render unstinting devotion—heart, mind, soul, and strength—to the Unseen? How can God, the great Unknown, be thus loved? For this to be *fait accompli*, it is entirely up to divine initiative. Saintly mystics know the rush when God takes over. For the rest of us spiritual pedestrians, the commandment to love totally is at least a start in the process; a target to aim at, a value hoped for, a direction. We believe Jesus to have sounded the depths of this affection in his relationship with his Father. He no doubt sensed the difficulty for others to experience the same intensity of his sentiment, so he linked loving God with loving the neighbor and oneself. And so, God is loved only as much as one's worst enemy.

When you are good to me, it is no trick to be good to you. But when you are a cad? . . . I can love me when I am brave, but when I'm a coward? . . . That is precisely when benevolence to me is needed most. That is why love is a commandment. Even under pressure, to try it is to like it. John's words sing with the buoyancy of the understanding heart. Churchgoers who do not make caring for others and self the point of their lives, miss the point. "Anyone who says he is walking in the light of Christ, but dislikes his fellow man, is still in darkness" (1 John 2: 9).

Alas, history's ruthless replay is a tragic saga of man's inhumanity to man. Human beings are simply not very good at loving their fellow humans. In his book *Humanity*, Jonathan Glover writes how the system of depersonalization induces an indifference to the enemy's humanness, so that the barbarism of war can prevail. At his court martial after the My Lai massacre, Lt. John Calley testified: "An enemy I couldn't see, I couldn't feel and I couldn't touch: nobody in the military system ever described the enemy as anything other than communism. They didn't give it a race, they didn't give it a sex, they didn't give it an age." Glover further asserts that Mao, with Marxist chill, was "willing to lose 300 million Chinese people in the atomic war. This would be half the population but would be no great loss as the country would always produce more people." Life is cheap but for the Great Commandment!

Regard means "to look at." What I become aware of takes a place inside of me. It is no longer an other, an object. Looking and seeing unites the observer and the observed. Two antagonists paid attention to each other and became useful neighbors. Together they won the 1993 Nobel Peace Prize: F. W. DeKlerk and Nelson Mandela. This could happen to Croats and Serbs, Arabs and Jews, Hutus and Tutsis, North and South Ireland.

In a 1990 conversation with the Dalai Lama, an American psychologist stumped his Tibetan Holiness with a familiar modern expression, "low self-esteem." Though the Dalai was fluent in English, he had no clue as to the meaning of "low self-esteem." It was an unknown concept in Tibet. Tibetan culture is dedicated to social courtesy, personal consideration and serviceable concern for one another. With this importance that Tibetans freely give each other, no native can feel insignificant. Poor self image cannot survive where attentive civility is a way of life. The Dalai concluded, "My religion is kindness."

To love God is to love His world. The world as it is, the bitter with the sweet. It admires the rose, and does not curse the thorn, nor does it caress it. It respects it. It listens to life. It expects only what is and asks for nothing, but is open to everything.

For the lucky ones, to fall in love is finally to confront one's realist self. Self-absorption starts to wane, along with pretense. Caring for another automatically expands the carer beyond self-centeredness. The mystery of loving unfolds—God happens . . . no need to seek Him. He is as close as the one beside you. An ancient Persian proverb says it all:

> I sought my God, my God I could not see.
> I sought my soul, my soul eluded me.
> I sought my neighbor, and I found all three.

MITE BUT MIGHTY

In this First Kings excerpt, the prophet Elijah strikes the note of a callused caller ordering pizza. He appears to take advantage of his prophet position by imposing his wants on a reverent and indigent widow. But then, generous hospitality has ever been a sturdy eastern tradition, even among the poverty stricken. Sometimes insensitive clergy exploit this benefaction.

The gospel has Jesus excoriating religious show-offs and the pitiless extortion of conscientious believers. Even today, unscrupulous evangelists have not ceased to prosper from an unsuspicious following. He does, however, endorse church donations, as he recommends the virtue of the impoverished widow's contribution of two coins, worth about one-fifth of a penny—all she had.

The largesse of the faithful to their church has been consistently legend. I recall an Ohio parish family of nine. The father was a laborer for the county at a very modest wage. They struggled to make ends meet, but they agreed to tithe. Every payday, right off the top, ten percent went to the church. But they never missed a meal or an installment on a bill. All seven children went to college. Their unselfish liberality had been bounteously blessed.

Write-off or not, people are usually serious about giving to charity. Once given however, subsequent appeals maturate to monuments of junk mail. Father Ernie Brainard shared this predicament years ago in the Oakland diocesan weekly, *The Voice*: "I once sent $5 to a Save The Whale group," he said. "I like whales. They are huge, amiable, playful mammals that sing joyfully in their watery dwelling. They revel in blowing water into the air and pounding the sea with their titanic tails . . . never have I met a vindictive whale . . . they practice the live and let live motif." What Father Brainard got for his five bucks was a whale of a surprise: "Shortly after my meager contribution, I was put upon to save the condor, the yellow-nosed salamander, the pink-eyed earthworm, the pigeon-toed sloth, the red-rumped shrike and the shrinking violet." The pester deserves a jester!

Philanthropy comes in assorted categories. Take Brian Bruckbauer, for instance. When he was ten years old his family went to Jamaica, West Indies, on vacation. An avid soccer player, he watched young Jamaicans play the game. Having brought his soccer ball with him, they invited him to join in. A real soccer ball was a luxury for them to kick around, since they were making do with old bottles and taped-up cardboard boxes. Brian let them keep his ball; when he got home he decided to take action. He collected 23 balls and delivered them to the Jamaicans. Later two hundred balls went to them along with pumps, cleats and jerseys. The benevolence has grown nationwide.

While possessions are not the lot of everyone, each human being is a separate treasure available to an emotionally hungry world. Everyone has founts of patience, gentleness, and understanding to share with the tired, the lonely, and the dispossessed. We surprise ourselves sometimes at the powerful impact of a simple, momentary courtesy.

Prior to WWII, for ten years a Maryknoller toiled in a remote China province. With his own hands he built a chapel, school and clinic. He was dearly loved. Then, the dread Japanese invasion occurred. Days and nights of incessant shelling reduced his mission to rubble. He was heartsick, exhausted from the sleepless nights of terror, but the worst was yet to come. As troops occupied the area, he was too spent to care if he lived or died. Bayonet in his back, a soldier prodded the missioner to pick up his meager belongings and move into file. Death on the spot would have been welcomed. For him life was over. But the priest decided to reach for the impossible—a smile for the enemy! So moved was the surprised soldier that he picked up the padre's bundle and politely escorted him to a place in line.

Burnout is washout for the oppressed who succumb. In this void, the victim feels that there is precious little to give. But even a little is a lot when given with the heart of the gospel widow. Anyone can run out of gas . . . but when the fuel gauge registers "empty," there is still a gallon in the tank!

FINAL CURTAIN?

Gazing at the gentle photograph of a seated Pablo Casals bending over his beloved cello, one can almost hear the melody he is playing. So moved by his music, the legendary photographer, Yousouf Karsh, arranged a pose he had never requested from a subject before or since. He asked that the cellist not face the camera, but just play.

In the Boston Museum of Fine Art where this photo is exhibited, an elderly gentleman daily stood motionless before the photograph in rapt attention. Observing this routine day after day, the curator finally approached the devoted beholder and inquired, "Why?" "Hush, young man, hush, I am listening to the music," was the reply he received.

This incident, reported in November 2000 issue of *Connections*, suggests a useful way to better understand the Bible. That is, not to face the words head on—literally, but to see beyond them to their meaning. It is like not fixing on the lyrics of a song in order to better hear its melody. The Bible is limited by language. The written word is ever an inconstant variable in any communication. What its writers meant when they wrote what they wrote, scholars have given their lives to decipher. The Bible can be seen as an impressionistic painting, highlighting the artist's insights. The canvas is not a photograph. To emphasize a momentous message, ancient authors employed a literary technique known as "apocalyptic writing." This device uses extreme, exaggerated language to make a point. This is similar to a person accentuating a pledge by adding the apocalyptic words "until hell freezes over." The language is inflated and not to be taken literally.

Mark is writing around 70 A.D. Jerusalem lay in ashes, the Temple is dust. The Jewish world was falling to pieces. The new Christians had bloody persecution to look forward to, but deliverance was expected in the second coming of the Lord. Mark had Jesus himself foreseeing this event and appears to put the foreboding words of the prophets in his mouth, as he predicts dire calamities of a world winding down. Pagan cultures were also gripped by such baleful forecasts, as the Sibylline Oracles attest. But it is difficult to associate Jesus with these scare tactics. He seems to put a positive spin on the ominous warnings by introducing the fig tree figure. Whatever the barren winter of discontent, its leaves promise a fruitful summer. It can be another way of saying that with God, disaster is never the bottom line. So, faithful people, do not lose heart—Providence is on the job. Our God is the God of a second chance!

Here is a second-chance story that appeared years ago in a San Francisco newspaper. On a warm clear day, 28-year-old Kenneth Baldwin stood mid-span on the Golden Gate Bridge and said good-bye to the world. His decision to kill himself somehow elated him. He gripped the guardrail, vaulted over the bar, and plunged more than 240 feet toward the frigid waters and what he believed would be certain death. In his own words:

> When I got to the bridge I believed I had made the right decision . . . And I felt more happiness than I had experienced for months. But I panicked when I pushed off and saw my hands leave the guardrail. I instantly knew I had made a big mistake, but there was nothing I could do but live through those agonizing seconds knowing I would be gone as soon as I hit the water.

But Kenneth Baldwin didn't die. Despite the 1-in-100 chance to survive the impact, he was not only alive and virtually unharmed after the ordeal, but treading water with a renewed vigor for life. "I should have died. But I didn't," he said. "And today, all I know is that I'm thrilled to be alive."

End-of-the-world scenarios have ever fascinated preachers. The dullest of them can wax eloquent on the spooky text: "The sun will be darkened, and the moon will not give its light, and the stars will be failing from the sky, and the powers of the heavens will be shaken." Preachers can feel a distorted illusion of power by alarming people. Every generation has its self-styled soothsayers prophesying the planet's demise. In upstate New York, William Miller insisted doomsday would be 20 March 1843. Scores of followers sold everything, donned white gowns, climbed a hill, and shiveringly waited to be the first to greet the Lord "coming amid the clouds" at first light. When nothing happened, they showed up on the same date again the following year. 1920 was the year of the Lord according to Judge Joseph Rutherford and his Jehovah's Witnesses.

To some scientists a "runaway universe" is not too farfetched; what with supernova explosions, global warming, the greenhouse effect, and ozone layer damage . . . not to mention seven decades of nuclear threat. They report energies permeating space beyond current knowledge. Astrophysicists maintain that our crucial main star, the sun, has about five billion years to go. Then it will expand immensely and burn out, taking with it the planets of its solar system, including Earth. Still, this is not the end of the cosmos, since our solar system is a mere speck among measureless galaxies.

So, what to think about the biblical Day of the Lord? Will He be coming for our scalps, or like a lurking traffic cop to surprise us with an eternal traffic ticket? Whatever the blazing imagery of the scripture, when he comes, just judge that he is, surely he will see how we have tried to love him.

POLL POLITICS

In 1925, when kings were losing popularity contests worldwide, Pope Pius XI solemnly declared Christ the King for the universal Church. Though never interested in that title, according to synoptics Matthew, Mark and Luke, Jesus was nevertheless executed for precisely claiming it. Pilate seemed amused to apply it freely to the battered defendant, to the obvious infuriation of the scorned Sanhedrin. He thought it a good joke on the haughty Hebrews to name a mangled crucified corpse as their king.

Revered colleague, Father Bill O'Donnell, of St. Joseph the Worker, Berkeley, CA, also had a hard time assigning kingship to Jesus, as he wrote in his 1991 parish bulletin:

> If I were king I'd eliminate the title, especially from Jesus' name. Kingship is one of those abominable inventions the powerful concocted to keep people enslaved. Just look at what kings have done to Ireland . . . the colonies . . . King David of the Israelites was scandalously corrupt and he was one of the good ones.

A similar sentiment was expressed in the Old Testament by Samuel, the last of Israel's Judges, when the people pleaded for "a king like those of other nations."

> If you insist on having a king like those of other nations he will conscript your sons and make them run before his chariots, some will be made to lead his troops into battle, while others will be slave laborers. They will be forced to plow in the royal

fields and harvest his crops without pay. He will take a tenth of your harvest and distribute it to his favorites. You will shed bitter tears because of this king you are demanding (1 Sam. 9).

In the Book of Judges, chapter eight, the victorious general, Gideon, is offered the crown. "But Gideon replied: 'I will not be your king, nor shall my son; the Lord is your king.'" And didn't "king" prove to be a dubious benefit for an Israel that prided itself on being a league of tribes with a great deal of local freedom and equality, since their rights were rooted in the covenant with Yahweh.

Back to politics and procurator Pontius Pilate! His charge, as it is today, was a much troubled land. Palestine was considered a backwater nuisance to Rome. Second-class provinces only rated procurators to govern in Caesar's name. The first was assigned to Palestine by Augustus when Jesus was six years old. Pilate took over when Jesus was 26 and ruled indifferently for about ten years. According to Jewish historians Philo and Josephus, he was contemptuous of Jewish religious customs, thus aggravating civil unrest and the seeds of sedition. Public tumult was dealt with quickly and severely.

John's Gospel features a puzzling dialogue between Pilate and Jesus. Some critics doubt that it even took place, since Jews enjoyed no legal right before a Roman tribunal. According to the noted New Testament scholar, the late Raymond Brown, the evangelist aimed at lifting Jesus above an itinerant preacher to the status of divinity. Hence royalty was appropriate for Jesus, which in John, he does not deny. However perplexing, the scene John describes is singularly dramatic. In an attempt to clarify this exchange, the Johannine account is herewith paraphrased hypothetically in today's idiom.

Pilate (bored with having to deal with another Jewish religious nut): Are you the king of the Jews?

Jesus (inwardly—let's get the question straight): Are you asking from your personal curiosity, or are you repeating local gossip?

The tables are turned; Pilate is now on trial.

Pilate (really roiled): Am I a Jew? Your own people have turned you in—what is your crime?

Jesus: Your kingdom has nothing to fear from me. Mine is out of this world.

Pilate: Then you are king.

Jesus: That's your word for it. Royalty for me is saying it like it is. Whoever appreciates what is—facts, reality, God's truth—understands me.

They are talking on two different levels. Pilate emphasizes the power of the state; Jesus, the power within honest people. Samuel Adams articulated the issue when he said, "We may look to our armies for our defenses, but virtue is our best security."

It is not hard to sympathize with Pilate. Responsible for keeping the lid on the Palestinian powder keg, he nonetheless seeks to set Jesus free. He passes the buck to Herod—to no avail. He ventures the choice of liberating Barabbas or Jesus—another stymie. Maybe scourging will get Jesus off his back . . . dead end! The Ethiopian Church canonized these efforts by naming June 25th St. Pilate's feast day.

Pilate was a politician who played the polls. He sold out to the public, not to principle. Though it is important for the civil administrator to know what the people are thinking, it is a mistake to make their opinion a core value.

We have played the Pilate part whenever our job took precedence over justice; the party over principle; petulance over pity; whenever we withdrew from a tough decision, or washed our hands of a mess that needed cleaning up.

History is not clear about Pilate's ending. He could have been remembered for the sentence of deliverance to the Unjustly Condemned, instead of the terrible words that have echoed through the centuries: "and he suffered under Pontius Pilate."

Index A
LITURGICAL CALENDAR
(Cycle B)

Index B
SCRIPTURAL REFERENCES

The Now Testament

About the Author

Joseph M. Wadowicz, appointed Monsignor in 1969 by Pope Paul VI, was born 1 October 1919 in New York. He earned his bachelor's degree at St. John's University in his home state and later received a Master of Divinity from St. Mary's in Baltimore, Maryland.

In 1945, Monsignor Wadowicz was ordained at St. Patrick's Cathedral by Cardinal Spellman. His pastoral activity following ordination included campus ministry at Ohio University. He also served at this time as a retreat director, editor and radio/television programmer.

In 1950 Monsignor Wadowicz was commissioned as a chaplain of the U.S. Navy. He served aboard several aircraft carriers and with the U.S. Marines and was later ranked Captain.

At Veterans Hospital in Martinez, California, Monsignor Wadowicz designed and directed a master's degree program in Pastoral Counseling. This was achieved in conjunction with the Graduate Theological Union of Berkeley, California. He was certified as a full acting supervisor of Clinical Pastoral Education a few years later.

At present Monsignor Wadowicz is pastorally active in Orange County, California. He is also hard at work on Cycle C of *The Now Testament*.